FOURTEEN
Autobiography of an Age Group
1965
The first edition was reviewed widely in UK, the Commonwealth, USA and, in translation, Italy.

'The results...are striking. Free from literary decoration, they have the vivid, direct reportage of *cinéma vérité*: the children make their ordinary experiences exciting, their extraordinary ones matter-of-fact', *Sunday Times*.

'As valid a piece of research as any academic or official pronouncement... the general public would (also) find it enlightening', *Times Educational Supplement*.

'Mr Measham has the rare ability to unlock the memory and imagination of young people...This book is a refreshing comment on the thoughts of teenagers today', *Tribune*.

'...a delightful selection from autobiographical essays by secondary modern children...who exhibit that astonishing precision of touch that traditional teaching usually destroys', Peter Worsley, *Guardian*.

'The book is a vindication of the freer approach to the teaching of English', *Times Literary Supplement*.

'For anyone interested in children the collection gives a valuable imaginative glimpse in depth of the world of the 14-year-old', David Holbrook, *Glasgow Herald*.

'...Authentic glimpses into the thinking world of young adolescents: the things that move them; the importance of the peer group; the desire for responsibility; the gradual widening of horizons; the opportunities sought in human relationships', *Sydney Education Gazette.*

'... has an ingenuous vitality which suggests that the sophisticated "pop persona" has no currency when the child's whole being is engaged. The children are content and often delighted to identify themselves with mundane family tensions and ordinary friendships', *The Use Of English.*

'The work illustrates the expressive power to which children can attain through minimal formal criticism. An interesting product of the "children's writing movement" in the British schools', *Child Development, USA.*

'D C Measham, an understanding and perceptive teacher in a British secondary school has given us all a warm and touching view of young people. In vigorous straightforward style, the authors unfolded their stories, and the result is now a lovely little book', *Chicago Daily News.*

*

The Italian edition *Quatordicenni* (translation by Maria Gloria Parigi) was published by the Nuova Italia Press as number 227 of the series 'Educatori antichi e moderni', with a prefatory essay by Gianni Rodari. It was reviewed by the following:
Reforma della Scuola, Rinascita, Trenta Giorni, Ricerche Pedagogiche, Terzo Ponte, Corriere di Napoli, Tempo Sereno, Ragazzi Enaoli, Paese Sera, L,Ora, L'Educatore Italiano, Liberta, La Voce Repubblicana, Tempo Medico, La Scuola Media, Orientamenti Pedagogici, La Ricerca, Il Giornale dei Genitori, Domenica del Corriere, Genova Notte, Corriere della Sera, La Naziione, Radio Svizzera Italiana.

FOURTEEN REVISITED

Fourteen: Autobiography of an Age-Group,
1965

with additional material
including a
1990 Afterword
and a
2008 Preface

Donald Measham

Lulu 2009

Fourteen, collected and edited by D C Measham
First published in 1965 by
Cambridge University Press.
LIBRARY OF CONGRESS
CARD NUMBER: 65-19146
Copyright reverted to D C (Donald Charles) Measham in 1991.

Reissued by Donald (Charles) Measham
with additional material as

FOURTEEN REVISITED

First published 2009

Copyright © Donald Measham

The right of Donald Measham to be identified as the author of this work has been asserted by him in accordance with the Copyright, Designs and Patents Act of 1988.

All rights reserved. No part of this publication may be reproduced, stored or transmitted in any form or by any means, electronic, mechanical or otherwise, without the prior written permission of the copyright owner.

ISBN 978-1-4092-6279-4

CONTENTS

Reviews and Reactions	1
Preface: *The Sixties*	7
Introduction	9
Section One	11
The Principal Contributors	82
Note	83
Section Two	87
Note	110
Conclusion	113
Afterword 1990	115
And 2008	117

The text of the autobiographies is re-set from that of the Cambridge University Press first edition of *Fourteen*, 1965. The 1960s reviews are collected here for the first time. All other material bears a date.

PREFACE: *The Sixties*

The reviews on the first two pages provide an incidental glimpse of Sixties attitudes; another side of the frivolous decade: its earnestness, its openness, its innocence. Also its acceptance of social pigeon-holing.[1] The fourteen-year-olds writing their autobiographies were 'secondary modern children'.

The Education Act of 1944 had set up a system – after the fashion of the tripartite society of Plato's *Republic* – where top tier performers in 'eleven-plus' tests were labelled 'academic', and (confusingly for Americans) required to attend grammar schools. Technical schools were for the second tier; 'secondary moderns' for the undistinguished majority.

Proposals intended to humanise the 1944 Act were in the air – and on the ground: Stuart Mason's 'Leicestershire Plan', for example[2]. While, at the 'chalk-face', there was the recurring discussion of whether teachers were artisans or professionals. A key notion within which was the ideal of teacher control. A brave new examination for all children of secondary school age – with course work components – called the CSE (Certificate of Secondary Education) was on its way; and Teachers' Centres and branches of NATE (The National Association for the Teaching of English) were springing up.

So there were plenty of idealistic English teachers, though their good intentions should have carried a Health-Warning. Chronic over-work and inter-school confusion arose

---

[1] My own remarks in Section Two about more and less 'academic' children are badly dated.

[2] Whereby grammar schools would become Sixth Form colleges teaching a broader curriculum, with secondary modern and junior schools reorganised to provide comprehensive education for the middle years.

from self-inflicted innovations such as peer-group moderation. Many hours were spent pursuing the ideal CSE syllabuses, specific to the individual school — the 'Mode C', a rallying call.

Yet by the mid-seventies, localness no longer seemed a virtue: in 1986 CSE was reintegrated with GCE O Level. Two years later, centralism was confirmed through the introduction[3] of a National Curriculum. That has meant — yes — levelling up, but also loss. Standardisation of the educational experience has, for instance, made individual projects of the *Fourteen* kind impossible. Its autobiographies were a response to a challenge, to their authors and the group – not a lust for grades. Work was assessed only in the sense that it was (valuably) 'shared.'

Another dichotomy apparent in the reviews (besides grammar/modern children) is that between 'traditional' and 'free' ways of teaching English. Subject-Predicate analysis always was absurd. I worked on syntax, taught inductively; the starting point being the typical English sentence: SVC, subject + verb + further information. All departures from that structure have a cause and a purpose; as in the differences between, say, 'You get up' and 'Up you get'. And I showed — taught — the children ways of persuading and arguing within set verbal markers. Children need help with structure and they need some labels. The baby had not really been thrown out with the bath water.[4]

Donald Measham

Matlock, December 2008

---

[3] The School Board of Victorian England also had a required national curriculum. Its derided schedules provide sensibly for a more literate work force.

[4] True of many others, though see D C Measham, *English Now and Then*, 1965. Through my grand children I sense the present National Syllabus's treatment of English mechanics may be quite successful. One of them became very interested in the ellipsis!

INTRODUCTION

Mr Vicars Bell has described an early lesson of his when he brought a mouse to school and set the children to write about it. Mr David Holbrook has had children record the delights of apples while munching windfalls. Mine was a simpler course—I asked the boys and girls to write their life stories. Nevertheless, in the same way, vigorous writing came from immediately available experience: they were not faced with the problem of *what* to write.

All the material in this collection was produced during the Autumn terms of 1961 or 1962 by the third year of a secondary modern school—a new school in a semi-rural area where parental occupation varied from borough engineer and stockbroker's clerk to nurseryman and 'chassis-straightener'.

Section 1 of the book consists of extracts from the children's writing, so arranged that the work can be read almost as if it were a single 'life'. In this way, one gets the feel of 'typical' childhood. However, boys and girls whose work appears more than once have been listed at the end of the section. Thus the book may be read also as a series of individual life stories. This process is taken a stage further in Section 2, where two complete autobiographies are reproduced as they were written.

Section 1, itself, is untouched by teacher's hand—except that I have standardised the spelling. Also, I have added the odd full-stop or comma where the passage was ambiguous—never to produce a new effect or to brisken an ambling style. I have made a few cuts, but in no case such as would alter the sense or produce entertainingly misrelated ideas; nor have the passages been rearranged internally in any way.

For readers who would like to know more about the background of the work, I have supplied a note at the end of each section.

D C M

Matlock College of Education, March 1965

SECTION ONE

1   *Janet.* I have no difficulty in starting my autobiography for the first five years of my life are just blank to me.

2   *Pauline.* One thing I remember being told that might be as good as anything for a beginning was when my father got hold of me and held me on his hand and said, 'Another white wedding to save up for, I suppose.'

3   *Linda.* Two minutes before Big Ben struck noon, I was born in Bethnal Green Hospital on the 12th May 1948. Trust me to be born at dinner time, although I don't remember getting any dinner.

4   *Eunice.* Fourteen years ago my mother attended Folkestone clinic, for inside her was a wriggling baby about to be born, ME. On the 6th November 1947 my mum went to Folkestone hospital and on 20th November I was born punctually at 6.30 p.m. when all the nurses were listening to the Queen's wedding on the wireless.

5   *Geraldine.* My mother, father and one-year old brother were living in a house with three storeys in Tottenham. Sharing the same house was my Aunt and Uncle (my mum's sister) with their two daughters, Susan aged four and Ann aged nearly three months. My mum was rather cross that her sister had beaten her to the second child, but really inside her I don't think she minded one bit because I'd be the youngest and most probably spoilt and looked after by everyone.

6   *Marilyn.* The Human Race Plus One: The 'plus one', me, came into being one rather typical Monday morning. Pelting rain,

thunder, lightning and hail. The time 9.15 — to be born on a Monday morning runs in the family, so I have been told.

From St John's Hospital, Chelmsford my mother sent my dad a telegram saying I was born. My dad couldn't come to the hospital because he was at home in bed, with chicken pox.

7   *Brian.* Four years before my birth my mother and father were married in a church on the Arterial Road near the Cricketers Public House.
The day was in 1943; my dad has never forgiven himself for marrying. It is the worst thing in the world you know he says.

8   *Pat.* In 1948 on the warm sunny day of the 25th February, at about twelve midday, I was born. What a shock for mother. We were then living in a small prefab in Vaughan Terrace, East Lane, North Wembley, Middlesex.

My brother was then only two years old and my sister was not even thought of. My mother tells me occasionally what a lovely baby I was and also how I have changed.

9   *Jane.* I was born in a bungalow at the top of an unmade road. The date was 13th May 1948. My two granddads had a bet, Granddad Black said I was going to be born on his birthday which was the 12th, Granddad Walsh said I was going to be born on the 13th, so he won.

10   *Nicholas.* It was a cold foggy day, December the seventh 1948, when I made an increase in the population. I was born at six o'clock and my mum says that I have never failed to turn up for tea ever since.

There was no discussion of a name when I was born in Stechford Hospital, it was a foregone conclusion because Nicholas Gregor has been the name given to the first son for several generations. One of the first Gregors was Scottish, but I don't want to end up like him, he was burnt at the stake.

11   *Lynne.* Being born in Holborn which is right in the heart of London the first light I saw was probably a smoky one. I can't really remember much till the age of three or four, when we lived in a big old house in Tavistock Place. There was a big basement downstairs and a light was on from seven till eleven.

12   *Maureen.* I was born on Tuesday October 26th 1948; at ten past eleven in the morning, at Stechford hospital, I weighed 6 1b 10 oz. At birth I was a most unusual baby, because the doctors just could not get me to cry, they gave me special treatment but this was in vain, in fact I didn't cry with tears until I was about three.

13   *Richard.* At two o'clock in the morning on a day with freak rain and wind storms I was born in a London hospital. I weighed the pretty average weight of 7½ lb. It was 1948 on the 24th February that I was born, and as I look back now I know my parents must have had it pretty hard. The war had just ended and the Korean war was just beginning, we had been bombed out once and work was hard to find. The home I came to was in Cable Street, Stepney.

     Our house was our own with three others. We acquired them from a former landlord who knowing my father left them for him in his will. The houses were in need of a great deal of repair, and as my father did not have the capital to repair and rent them he had to get rid of those that were not in use. So he sawed through the rafters and called the public inspectors in. When they had seen them the wheels of demolition started to move.

14   *Kevin.* When I was born I had a big pram, but then mum and dad decided to take me for a holiday. So they had to get a smaller one it was big enough to lie down in and it had a hood and rain cover but it folded up.

We reached Lowestoft without any troubles. Then we had to get a taxi to Gorton, the driver put the pram on the rack without tying it on.

We were sailing along merrily when we came to a forked road. The taxi shot round one corner and the pram shot off the top and round the other.

15   *Raymond.* My father was just being demobbed, the war had been over about two years. I was born in Ireland, in Belfast to be exact, in Harleston Street, three hundred yards from the River Lagan.

The first drink I had was half a cup of warm sugar water, which I drank thirstily, so my mother said. She said also that I was a very awkward baby who had to be forcibly fed by the nurse who did so by ramming a bottle down my throat, after holding my nose and waiting until I opened my mouth for air. She would hold me there until I had sucked the last gramme from it.

After six weeks I moved to London where I caught bronchitis and was sent to hospital, this was my first close shave for I very nearly died.

When it was near Christmas and the ground was covered in snow, my mother would wheel my pram over Hampstead Heath and load my four-wheeled transport with snowballs to throw at my father coming home from work.

My father was late home from work that day so consequently my feet grew steadily colder. I began to cry, so my mother threw the snowballs away. Just as soon as she had done this dad came round the corner. So he reached home unsnowballed and I got cold feet as a consolation.

16   *Susan*. The first thing I can remember when I was a child is when I was about eighteen months old to two years when I went on holiday with my parents. We went to Ramsgate.

There was a glut of peaches that year and therefore they were very cheap. My father bought some of these lovely sweet juicy things with the soft furry outside. The peach that I was given was so big that as I held it in two hands and took a bite out of it you couldn't see my face at all, just hair. I kept biting and biting the peach then, suddenly I bit something hard, it hurt my teeth. I started crying, my father took the peach away from me and my mother took me out of my pram and cuddled me.

Next I was told that the peach I had loved was bad and it was thrown away before my very eyes, thus I began to cry again and the only thing that stopped me crying was another peach.

17   *Ray*. One day Dad was walking across the lawn, I shouted 'Charge' as I ran full speed at him. When I got within a couple of feet of him I had a strange sensation, then I realised he had got me by the ankles and was dangling me just over the ground. Then Dad started to use me like a yoyo and I couldn't stop laughing, so then he threw me over his shoulder. I was only lodged on so I began to slip, so he put me down on the ground. Then I began to follow him as he walked on. All of a sudden I clutched at his leg. I held it with both arms and I twisted my leg around his, but he kept on walking until I found it most uncomfortable and let go.

As we were walking down the garden I kept on trying to twist dad's arm, we were now nearing the shed. Dad once again grabbed me by the ankles and turned me upside down, then he walked to the shed and dangled me over the water. There were four goldfish in the water-butt and when they came up for air and opened their mouths you could see inside, it looked like a coal mine on fire.

18   *Maureen.* As I didn't like bread very much nanny would get a slice of bread, and say to me to take a bite and we will make a pattern, then take a bite from another side, this would continue until there was no pattern and no bread left.

At the age of four, little nanny died, I did not understand this at the time as I was told she had gone away, but we still continued to live at 'Alberta' with grandfather; as I followed him about everywhere, we found we were good company for each other.

19   *Nicholas.* I can vaguely remember my Great Grandmother and her (what I now know as) Victorian bric-a-brac. I can remember the shelves and glass cabinets full of ornaments covered in dust. The bungalow always had a heavy, stuffy atmosphere with a distinctive smell. It was full and overcrowded with furniture and I remember clearly the large oak table with a thick purple tablecloth and its fringe almost touching the ground. The wire-netted fireguard which I often used to place my fingers in stands out clearly in my mind.

The jackdaw in her garden was popular with all relations and is also clear in my mind. The jackdaw used to talk saying 'Hallo Jack, hallo Jack' and there was a robin's nest in her shed.

But above all this mess she did the most wonderful embroidery she played the piano very well and painted a variety of pictures. The only time the bungalow was clean was when the piano tuner came and there was always a big fuss.

The other of my Great Grandmothers always liked to tell stories to her great grandchildren. One of her favourite stories she liked to tell was when she lived on a farm in Somerset and how she went to church on horseback when she got married. My Great Grandfather was alive but I don't remember him. The thing that puzzles me is how these two could have met and married when my Great Grandfather was the village blacksmith in Steeple, Essex and my Great Grandmother lived on a farm near Wookey Hole, Somerset.

20   *Paul.* The Blakes (from Australia) were the parents of my mother's brother's wife. This sounds somewhat complicated, but family relationships are just that. They arrived by taxi on Saturday because we did not know when exactly they were arriving and so could not meet them. We heard the taxi draw up outside and to the accompaniment of a deafening blast on a motor horn we rushed out to see if it was them.

Apparently Bella (Gran'ma Blake) had persuaded (with an extra half crown) the taxi driver to lean on his horn button until we came out. As we reached the gate the 'leaning' ceased and the taxi driver got out to help an enormous Bella to roll out of the car, followed by Gran'pa Blake a small man in an enormous hat. Bella dismissed the taxi driver and said 'Hello', also, as a side statement, she introduced her husband with whom I was busily making friends (because of the hat).

We went in to tea and from then on Bella hardly ever stopped talking. After we had heard all the news about our friends and relations 'down-under' we were told of Uncle Bill's beautiful house on a hill overlooking Sydney Harbour. Gran'pa Blake said 'Every room has panelling of a different Australian wood.' He also told us of Uncle Bill's car 'Bomb' and how he and my cousin Pat love speed and how Aunty does not so they blindfold her so that she cannot watch the speedometer.

21   *Doreen.* I never really enjoyed visiting my nana because she could only speak Welsh and I could only speak English and

after we had both said hello to one another I had to use my father or Aunt Mary as an interpreter which rather slowed up the conversation and the odd jokes. Nana was a very short woman with pure white hair and short stubby fingers that I have unfortunately inherited.

22   *Janet.* My Gran had been staying with us for about a week now and neither my sister or I knew why.
'Why is mummy so fat?' I asked. 'Janet, don't say that,' was the reply.

23   *Doreen.* Mrs Smith kept saying wouldn't you like a sister and I kept replying yes I would and didn't take any more notice.

24   *Paul.* Then one night mummy didn't come to say good night but dad did and said 'Paul, when you wake up in the morning we might have a present for you.' I could not guess what the present could be so I went to sleep.
In the morning at about 7.30 a.m. I woke up and dad told me to put on my dressing gown and some slippers and come and see what we had got. Dad gave me several hints and I hoped it was my gun-slick brother I was hoping for. I followed dad into the spare room and found mum lying in bed smiling, and did I find the 'Bat Masterson' brother? No! All I found lying in a carrycot was a tiny, pink, wrinkly, black-haired sister!

25   *Michael.* — My mother, father and I and my baby brother which I have not told about as he is not important because he got all the attention and I only lived with my mother and father...

26   *Valerie.* At this time there were eight girls and four boys in our family. At weekdays we all had our dinner at different

times because we came in at different times, but on Sundays we had it all together; the fourteen of us.

27   *Janice*. I can still remember the day I first learned how to whistle. I was about two and a half years old. Every day I would sit on my swing in the garden just blowing and blowing but it was no good.

Till one evening I was sitting up in bed trying when a tiny little peep came out. I was so excited I almost fell out of bed and ran into the living room to show Mum and Dad. They both sat looking at me and waiting. 'It will come in a minute,' I kept saying,... but it didn't. 'Never mind,' said Mum, 'perhaps it will come in the morning.'

28   *Valerie*. When I was three I broke a bottle, I drank out of a boat bottle, one of those with teats at both ends of it. We had at home a fairly low table which the bottle was on. I pushed it off and then until my mother bought another one I had to drink out of a sauce bottle with a teat on the end of it.

One time I was the only child in, I suppose the others had gone out. My mother was in the garden hanging some washing out and I was sitting in my high chair. I was fidgeting and suddenly the high chair fell over on to the floor. I screamed, as I always did when I hurt myself, and my mother came running. After a long cry I was all right besides a cut on the chin. Whenever I hurt myself I always cried without making a noise. I would sit or stand there without breathing and my mother always got very worried.

When I was just over two Janice was born. Again my mother had to go into hospital and again I saved my pennies.

29   *Doreen*. I was woken up at eight o'clock by Michael who was the eldest and Peter who said in a whisper,' Guess what

we've got a baby brother.' This didn't mean much to me at the time as I didn't really know what he meant, but I knew that I was supposed to be excited and I replied in my new language, 'mama' and got hold of the rungs of my cot and shook them so that the cot moved from side to side.

My brother was named David and after a few weeks I got used to him although he was still red and bald. I was about three at the time and had been given a brightly coloured ball that I could just hold in one hand.

30   *Geraldine.* When I was three, my brother, another girl my age and I went for a walk and John, being the boss took us to the golf-course and we got lost, but mum and dad found us not long after. A few months later we were playing with my friend Helen when my father called us saying, 'we've got a surprise in the house for you, come and have a look.'

When we arrived at the house he took us into the bedroom and there was my mum with a baby in a cot. I don't remember if I liked it then but I certainly don't like it now, it was a tiny little girl. Mummy had a list of names for girls which she had made out in hospital, but she couldn't choose so she asked us what we'd like to call it. John said he would like it to be called Joanna, I think that was the name of his little girl friend.

I didn't like this horrible little thing that was taking up all the time of Mum and Dad. She was spoilt and they didn't spoil me any more and they didn't love me any more or care about me. That's what I thought anyway, but they told me they did (they still tease me about it now). Slowly but gradually I became a bad-tempered, sulky-looking child. I began to get naughty and John who was a terrible shocker was taking me everywhere and getting us lost. One day when he had a new tricycle he ran away on it and we searched everywhere for him and as we couldn't find him we went down to the police station, to find him there eating cakes and drinking cokes.

31   *Janet.* On Christmas Eve while I was tucked up in bed at Chelmsford my mother had Ruth at 11.30 Christmas Eve. The best Christmas present anyone could wish for. Whilst dad was at home looking after Mum, he broke numerous cups and saucers.

32   *Lynne.* At the back of the house there was an outhouse, which contained a lot of valuable junk. There was a small garden which had a rockery at the end and one large wall, which surrounded a large block of brick almost like a prison called 'Peabody Buildings'.
        Now when it was hot I used to have an old tin bath filled with cold water, take it out on the lawn and swim the 400 yards in it. As it was a hot day I asked whether I could have it out.
        'No, not today,' said mum, 'it's too cold, go and play while I go and make the beds.'
        I wasn't satisfied and feeling rather naughty I got the tin bath out and filled it with water. Then I took my dress off so I just had my vest and knickers on and jumped in. It was lovely till I heard mum coming. I didn't know what to do, when suddenly without any thought I took a deep breath and stuck my head under water, thinking that because my head wasn't showing nowhere else was. I didn't realise my bottom was sticking right up into the air.
        I was going green blue and purple under the water and had to come up after five seconds. My mother was terribly cross and I was terribly sick after swallowing mouthfuls of water.

33   *Nicholas.* Whenever I walk past the lake in Prospect Park my eyes are drawn towards the row of rock-like stones at the edge of the lake. Then through the mist in my mind I get a

strange feeling that the lake should not only be much larger but also frozen. Then I see the picture of sea-gulls sliding across the ice as they make a pancake landing.

These memories come from the days when I was wheeled through the park in my pram during Winter. No doubt the line of stones which stands out so clearly in my mind, almost came level with my eyes at the side of the pram. These stones give me a kind of triumphant or pleasant feeling as in some remote way I remember trying to pull out some of the upholstery studs from the pram. Probably I eventually got one out as I looked at the rocks and somehow these two incidents have stayed together in my mind.

This happy feeling soon vanishes however, as in a vague sort of way the sound of a man whistling a tune that I now know as 'Greensleeves' came on the radio after I had arrived home from the park.

I can't figure out whether it was the actual tune that made me cry. Perhaps it was the connection at the same time of my mum going straight out of the back door with coat still on, and leaving me alone, only to appear again with her arms full of frozen stiff washing sticking out all around her.

I am not sure whether all these things happened on the same day, but I seem to associate them with a Monday. I still can't listen to 'Greensleeves' without feeling a sadness creep up inside me.

I must have been less than three years old because I am three years older than my brother and he would have occupied the pram after this age.

34   *Lucy*. I know once I was on my way home and I pushed the swing up and I forgot to run away and it hit me on my two front teeth. And for at least two weeks they kept on turning round and round, then they finally came out. Mother said that if

I put them under my pillow that night the fairies would come and take it away and give me some money.

There was another time when I called out when I was in bed that I wanted a drink of water. Mummy called out ' Go to sleep and I'll bring it up.' I thought at the time this was natural, then a few years later it suddenly dawned on me while I was in bed how could I go to sleep and then drink a glass of water.

35   *Jonathan.* My bedroom which I slept in with my brother was downstairs. It had two windows which are only of medium size, a fireplace which was hardly ever used, two doors, one an entrance to our bedroom and the other an entrance to our mother and father's bedroom. The room is only about fifteen feet square. We slept in a double bed in one corner.

One thing that often happened is we would be in bed all ready to go to sleep when I would hear 'zipp'. I would look at my brother, he would look quite normal so I would get back to trying to sleep.

A little later I would hear the same sound. I would then explore the bed with my feet to find out what was happening. My foot would come into contact with my brother's feet, then my toes would go into a hole in the sheet which my brother had made with his toes. After a few minutes' silence he would say that his foot got caught in a small hole and he pulled his foot and it made the hole even bigger. We would then turn over and go back to sleep.

36   *Helene.* I have lived all my life in Stonebridge, but it has changed a great deal over the thirteen years. Once it was just a village with a few houses dotted along Ferry Road. There was no Hillcrest Estate, no village hall and very few shops. Many more people live in the village now and there was once a time that we knew nearly everyone, but now I can go shopping and not meet

a soul that I know. Trees are cut down and bungalows go up. I live in a green belt, so we are not affected. There is a farm at the back of our house which has not been lived in since the farm labourer and his family moved on to another farm a little way up the road. It is still looked after, but most of the time is deserted; the pond is quiet, no children fishing in it, although the calmness is often disturbed by the cry of a moorhen, or the moo of a cow in the fields nearby. The farmhouse looks lonely, only the swallows visit it now every year to nest under the eaves.

Funny isn't it I didn't like passing an empty house, it made me feel ashamed. A house waiting to be lived in by a nice cosy family, well that is what I used to think, but now I can just walk by and not even notice that it's empty. The only house that still makes me feel like that is the farmhouse, most houses are not empty for long any more, but I know that this one will. In fact until it is pulled down or falls down, for it has no electricity and no bathroom.

I often take a glance at it as I go by, we had some good times there. The pond I fell in, the barns with secret hidy holes in which we so often played hide and seek, the air raid shelter and the trees overhanging it all bring back happy memories.

37   *Keith*. Where we used to live there were potteries all over there. The smell of the black smoke pouring out of the soot-covered chimneys. The work was from seven o'clock in the morning till five o'clock at night.

38   *Martin*. The Sussex fen was flat and soot black. It was bleak and desolate in Winter with patches of trees lining the horizon.

Our nearest neighbour lived a quarter of a mile away. The farmhouse was half wood and as black as the soil. The centre of the house dipped and was cracked like many of the houses in that area where even the strongest foundations moved.

Despite these conditions the soil itself was some of the most fertile in England and we had plenty of fuel for the fires as we dug up trunks of Bog Oak (wood that has been buried for several thousand years and has half turned to coal).

The farm-road was almost straight and at one end you could see a full mile to the other end. On one side of the road there is a dyke used for irrigation purposes. The water is run into it from a canal that ran crossways at one end. The dyke hadn't many bridges but one was almost opposite.

39   *Jim*. I used to go and play with my friends across the street for a little while. They had funny names for boys, but I did not play with them too often because they would jump on people's cars or let the tyres down. My mother did not like the two boys so she forbid me to play with them. Their mother would always have quarrels with the lady next door and one day their arguments led to a fight and they started pulling each other's hair out and ripping each other's clothes. This brought the whole street out but none of them interfered.

40   *Eunice*. I was very upset when the last of the house buyers went for they had bought with their money all my happiness of my early youth. But finer days were in store.

41   *Lynne*. The removal van was over an hour late, they had got stuck in a traffic jam in the City. At last all the furniture was loaded on and although the two removal men had trouble getting the sideboard upstairs we were ready to go.
I went round, silly but true, saying goodbye to the fireplace the window ledge and the old tin bath.

42   *Jean.* When I was three years old we moved to Ashley into a house almost opposite Doctor Brown, in between the Red Lion common and the police station. It had a beautiful big garden with many flowers. There were little paths right down the bottom of the garden with crocuses and flowers which look rather like bluebells but aren't, these flowers were round the edge of the paths. The people that lived there before had two geese and some canaries in an aviary which was outside.

43   *Malcolm.* One day we moved suddenly out of the blue for no one had told me. It was a Saturday and the removal men came, packing everything into tea chests. They chipped off practically all the paintwork. My dad called them clumsy -- -- -- (the dashes represent an evil word). Of course he only said this to the small one for the other was a massive chap who would have surely knocked his block off.

44   *Barbara.* At last we reached the Underground station, Nigger, our cat was scratching at the door of his basket. Dad got the tickets and we proceeded down the steps but of course dad's watch was slow and the train was in. We ran and ran, Nigger's basket going backwards and forwards, left to right. Just as we got in the porter shouted 'Mind the doors' and the train pulled out of the station.

45   *Malcolm.* The whole place smelt damp and of plaster. The garden can be easily described, it was literally a jungle. It was in such a state for nobody had lived there for almost two years.
       On arrival my brother Stewart and I naturally went into the garden to look around. There were twenty different trees in the garden and Stewart selected one and began to climb it. I was wandering about and suddenly heard a cry coming from the direction of Stewart. I went to him, he explained that his leg was

trapped between the two main branches. I could do nothing, so I left him to fetch my dad. Faint groans of agony floated from where he was.

With the aid of a rusty drain pipe we eventually prised his leg free, amid moans of despair. Stewart examined his leg.

After some time Stewart stopped limping. I saw this and said to him,' How is your leg?' He at once resumed limping saying, 'It's sheer agony.'

46   *Doreen.* In February we went to look at our new house. It was very big and once or twice I got lost but was always rescued by a little black scottie who led me to my mother. Besides being a very large house the only other thing that I thought unusual was a green, pale green, wash-basin and bath, both with brilliant red rugs that reminded me of some stuffed olives that I had seen that Christmas.

47   *Sue.* The garden of our house was very large (it was long rather than wide). The top was well-cultivated but somehow the bottom half never really got dug. I liked the bottom half best for playing around in. But the top was best for resting. At the very top was a beautiful plum tree that played arches with an apple tree.

48   *Jean.* The first Christmas at Ashley was a white one. In fact we were blocked in for a while by the fast-falling snow.

49   *Rita.* When I was four I was getting a doll and pram, and my brother a bicycle for Christmas. A few days after Christmas we had been naughty. When my Dad came home my mum told him. He said he was going to tell Father Christmas to take our presents back. We knew we had left them in the hall. My Dad

started shouting up the chimney, 'Father Christmas, take their toys back,' and we were yelling, 'No, Father Christmas, don't.'

When we went out into the hall all the presents had gone. We rushed back into the kitchen and shouted up the chimney, 'Please, Father Christmas, send them back.' We returned to the passage and there they were.

50   *Barbara.* You see, my mum was always moving the furniture around. Well, dad went to work after dinner and being the day the shops closed after dinner my mum was home. She was a bit bored, so she decided to move things round. The Christmas tree was by the window, so mum moved it to on top of the table by the door. It looked very pretty and the tree looked lovely with all the new decorations on it.   Dad got home at twelve o'clock after finishing work. He didn't know mum had moved the Christmas tree. Dad came upstairs and put his hand round the door to switch the light on and, crash, he knocked the Christmas tree to the floor. When he eventually got the light on he saw that almost all the tree decorations were broke. He didn't know what I'd say for he knew how I treasured my little tree and didn't even like someone going near it. Dad tried to pick up the tree, but it made such a crash when it fell that I got up and was standing just inside the door. When dad turned round and saw me he said,' Go back to bed, Barbara, that's a good girl.' 'What's happened to my tree?' I said and began to cry.

51   *Raymond.* I don't remember what my first Christmas was like as I was too young; but my second Christmas I remember waking up to find a large golden teddy bear peeping out of the top of my sack of toys. I played with this a lot and every time I was smacked I would run to find teddy for comfort. I would lie down on the settee and tell him that 'mummy smacked me and I don't love mummy any more.' It seemed to me that teddy would

wear a sympathetic face and he would say 'never mind, mummy didn't mean it.'

I have kept that teddy for twelve and one half years and now Shirley my little sister has it, but to her it will never be the same as it was to me.

52   *Christine.* I woke up as usual at four o'clock and unwrapped the parcels at the bottom of the bed. And jumped straight onto Mum, blowing whistles and shrieking my head off. After using dad as a bucking bronco for about five minutes I was packed off to bed and told not to make a sound till eight o'clock. So, after sorting through the booty at the bottom of the bed I selected some sweets and a cuddly toy and went back to bed.

We had my gran and granddad staying with us, now granddad was an early riser, so as soon as I heard him get up and go into the kitchen and put the kettle on, I crept out of bed, clutched as many of my precious presents as I could and toddled off to the kitchen. Granddad had lit a huge logfire and the kettle was boiling its head off. After we had wished each other merry Christmas I dragged the old kitchen chair (it was one of those huge old-fashioned things with wooden arms) up to the fire and sat there sorting out my presents and having a really good time. Then granddad asked me to go and find out whether everyone wanted tea or not. So off I trotted first to my uncle's room. I knocked on the doors because I didn't want to get told off and crept in to find out if they wanted tea; after being told to hop it as it wasn't time to get up. Well now I knew they weren't properly awake, so after bouncing on the end of the bed I tried again and received a mumbled yes. From there I went to mum's room. 'Grand —' 'I thought I told you to go back to bed.' 'I'm helping granddad. Do you want tea?' ' Oh well, yes.' So back I went to granddad, they all wanted tea. Everybody was up within an hour and so we got breakfast over.

At about ten o'clock my other gran, my uncle Joe, aunt Josie, Auntie Daisy and Uncle Albert came round to help cook the dinner. When it came to putting the bird in the oven we found it was too big. Now my gran who was supposed to be cooking it thought and said it was very funny and collapsed with laughter, so mummy carved off the legs and just managed to get it in. As a result we didn't get dinner till about three, but still it was a marvellous dinner. Nearly everybody went to sleep after the meal except for one or two who volunteered to wash up, but the best time was yet to come. That evening at about six o'clock there were streams of people coming into our house and somebody started to play the piano and there was a lot of laughter and noise. You could hear the noise clearly a block away.

After everybody had settled down we had what we call a fun and games period. My uncle did what he called his party piece where he would place a glass of water on a tray with another tray on top on which an egg was balanced, according to the rules uncle went out of the room and the egg was supposed to fall into the glass of water and for reasons best known to itself it never happened, five times he tried and five times it failed. My aunt sent six people out of the room and spread out some paper on which she spread cornflakes, the people were told there was a path between some eggs. They were blindfolded and told to walk through and oh the mess and the noise everyone not playing shrieked with laughter. Now at the time Johnny Ray was very popular, so dad complete with tears imitated Johnny Ray and ended up flat on the floor. Now I was beginning to get tired so I went and laid on the bed and slept.

53   *John*. One Christmas I recollect the school's small bring-a-jelly-party was visited by that majestic old gentleman Santa Claus.   He brought gifts of ice cream and sweets. Everyone

rallied round admiring his beard, and although one side was hanging off our belief in him was still unshakeably strong.

54   *Pauline.* The first time I went to school my mother came with my eight year old sister and myself. I remember standing at the bus stop waiting for the bus, I had my blue satchel over my head and one arm, in it I had numerous objects that I thought were to do with school. One was a Red Riding book about three inches high.

55   *Jack.* I was in Miss Mark's class and she was a very kind teacher. On the first day, I remember seeing my mother looking over a glass-topped door and waving good bye. When some of the children saw them go they started crying for their mothers. The teacher was kind and comforted them and showed this kindness all through the time we was there.

56   *Maureen.* The first day, being very brave in my new school uniform, I didn't cry, but I made up for it on the second day, I remember. I cried so much that the teacher let me sit on the foot rest of her big old-fashioned chair.

57   *Johnny.* Our parents were very worried about our education, so they tried to get both my brother and me into Ashley Primary school, but the headmaster whose name I cannot remember said the school was full and so we would have to go to Swinton. He said a coach would pick us up at the Hotel.
       On the way home from Ashley school my mother went into one of the village shops and while she was being served she asked where Swinton was. The answer was that it was about six miles out in the country. He later said that you didn't need a coach to get there but a helicopter.

58   *Rosemary*. One night the coaches did not turn up because of fog. We were standing waiting for half an hour before a telephone call came through telling us that the coaches had got lost in the fog. We all sat in the classroom playing 'Hangman' on the blackboard with a teacher, she had put a book title up and we were guessing, when another teacher walked in and said, 'Oh, "Alice in Wonderland"— oh!' realising then what she had done. Everybody sat there laughing. Later Mrs Clarke went to the little shop round the corner and bought a carrier-bag full of biscuits, which still only allowed us to have two biscuits each.
   At last round about five forty five the coaches turned up, although we still didn't arrive in Ashley until seven p.m.

59   *Patricia*. The first lesson we had was reading. We were each given a book which teacher said was called 'Janet and John'. I opened it at the first page where I saw a lot of little words. I could only read one of them and that was the word 'the'. I said to Linda, 'Can you read any of these words?'
   She replied,' Yes, only the word " her ", can you read any?
   ' I said, 'Yes, the word "the".'
   So I taught her the word I knew and she taught me the one she knew.

60   *Maureen*. All we did was played in the sandpit, played with plasticine or the counting beads; those who fancied themselves as artists drew pictures, as they were called with the fat crayons which we kept in one of our father's old tobacco tins.

61   *Barbara*. I was at school on the very first day and the teacher gave me a bottle of milk. A little shutter came across my throat. I just could not swallow the horrible milk.

62   *Brian.* At the age of five I started school like most other children. But in a different way for my mum, her got me up and marched me to school. At first I liked it but my mum left me and the heavens opened in my eyes. I looked and saw nobody else crying so I ran over to the door and started kicking it with my hands. It hurt so I stopped and began wailing. 'I want my mum,' I bawled. She appeared in the doorway. I ran up to her and said, 'Me's going to kick you for leaving me.' So I did and a big black bruise rose with dotted bits of blue and yellow here and there. But I settled down after all and played with a truck. But things started to get tiresome, so I started taking milk out of the crate and putting them under the odd table. Being fairly cunning I placed chairs all round the table, thus blocking it from view. Miss Nichols rang a little bell and said, 'Milk time.' She looked at the crate and saw three milks.

There was a big rush and big cries broke out from all. I appeared with a grand smile. The teacher said, 'What have you done with the milks?' I replied with a sniff and a sob, 'I've drunk 'em, miss.'

She looked under the odd table and saw five empties and two half which I did not feel like. But I was not forgiven by any means. I had to drink the other two which I had not finished. In the middle of which I broke out into violent coughing, but it was no use, she still kept pouring.

I coughed, I fought and I cried. When I finished the teacher stated 'you pupils would like a break I suppose. 'I went to pair up with my partner, but he backed off and cried,' I'm not having him as a partner, he's a milk drinker and a thief 'cause he didn't leave me a milk.'

63   *Helene.* Mummy took me to the cloak room where many other mothers and children were sitting or standing. Some were crying, some screaming and some just sat there and did not cry at

all, only stared at everyone that went past. I did not cry and I didn't stare either, just watched the mothers and children go in two by two and watched the mothers coming out, some looking rather lonely on losing their little helper and companion— who now would not go shopping with her in the morning, return home to cook the dinner, clean the house, have dinner and go out in the afternoon and help in the garden. Now she would only see her after school, at dinner-times and at week-ends.

The first night when I came home from school I got all my dolls and teddy-bears, lined them all up on the shelf, looked at them all one by one and said in a forlorn voice, ' I haven't got time for you any more.'

64   *Kevin.* When I was five I started school. I liked it quite a bit, but nothing much happened except a man was running towards the school gates, he tripped up and fell flat on his face, his hat went rolling on down the slope.

65   *Richard.* I remember one day when I was laid up with measles. I was four at the time and my eyes were very sore. It was about seven o'clock and I was lying on the black leather couch in our living room. My eyes were so sore that I was compelled to close them most of the time. When I did open my eyes I looked at the bright glowing mantle of the gas light that hung right above me. The chains that hung one up and one down from the gas light would occasionally strike each other making tinkling sounds. I remember too the radio playing in the background.

66   *Molly.* I was six and a half years old and my sister went down with measles. I had to keep away from her, but it didn't work because next week I was down with it, also I had pneumonia, the doctor said I didn't have a chance of living, my

mother sat by my bed-side day and night. I had all things done to me, it was dreadful, my sister got better, but I got worser (I always do).

About a week or two later the doctor said I had four hours to live, my mother wept, so did my sister. These four hours went quickly and quietly for me, soon the clock struck the fourth hour, the doctor said I would just have to try and pull myself through he could do nothing. I took my last breath and instead of dying I breathed on, the family around me gave a great sigh. The next thing I knew was that my mother was in hospital, suffering with tiredness and shock.

67   *Ken.* I was born at King George's Hospital on the 29th April 1948, I will always remember that because I went back there five years later to have my tonsils out. When I was informed I thought it was grand, I was dressed in my best suit and taken in my uncle's car, a big cumbersome Vanguard in battleship grey with red spots where rust had affected it and a preventative had been painted on.

The inside was musty and smelt ghastly, it had been a sunny day and the leather was red hot, the flower in the holder inside the window had shrivelled up and was drooping over the seat, even the velvet red devil in the back window had fallen off. I got in the front and took my usual cushion, (I could only see out of the window this way) and settled down for a comfortable ride.

68   *Barbara.* At the age of seven mum took me on a great trip to see Uncle Horace. He had never been seen by me and I know now that he has never been by anybody. Mum first said he would be at the Baker's Arms, so we went round to the bus stop and got on a bus which took us there. But alas when we got there he wasn't there and we had to get on another bus which took us to

outside Whipp's Cross Hospital where, mum said, Uncle Horace was a doctor.

69   *Jean.* That day we were not allowed any dinner and in the afternoon a nurse came in with injections, she gave my friend's doll an injection and then her, then the nurse went out of the room for about five minutes and then came back and gave my teddy one which I now know was not real. When the nurse gave me my injection I thought it was the longest needle in the world, it seemed so at the time.

70   *June.* Whatever they had in the syringe had started to work. I was sitting up (for the nurse was still doing my hair) and I felt my head fall forward, but how much I wanted to go to sleep I could not. I kept on telling myself that the nurse would not be long and I was right.

71   *Chris.* I remember just before going into the operating theatre which was on the fourth floor, I looked out of the window and all of a sudden from nowhere a great cloud of smoke rose. It was a hooter blowing, but no sound coming from it.

72   *Pam.* They took me in this room and I was laid on a trolley and then this man put this mask over my mouth and told me to breathe in deeply and then out, then he asked me to count. Then it seemed as if I was caught in a whirlpool. Next minute it seemed I was lying in bed with a sore throat.

73   *Maureen.* Soon after my seventh birthday, I used to go to play with a little boy down the street, we couldn't play proper games because he was only about six months old, I would amuse him with a rattle or a squeaky doll. I mainly went round there to

see his mum, she was one of my mum's best friends. I went round there almost every week day, but I remember one day as if it was yesterday. It was not a very nice day, Auntie Rose told me to go into the living room where she had lit a fire. She had a small gong which stood on the mantelpiece, I asked Auntie Rose if I could play with it. As she was in the kitchen she called back a reply of' Yes'.

So I put one foot on the hearth, one hand on the top of the mantelpiece to pull myself up. As I did this my foot slipped backwards and as there was nothing to hold onto, I fell face downwards straight on to the red hot coals. Luckily enough there was no flame, as I screamed and as I was dazed I didn't really feel too much pain. Auntie Rose rushed in and picked me up, before long Auntie Rose was crying with me. Not knowing what to do, she wrapped me in a blanket and ran with me all the way home. When we arrived at the back door, Auntie Rose stepped in and called to my mum, ' Lil, don't get worried, but Maureen has had an accident.'

When my mum saw me, she too started crying. My mum phoned up my dad from work and told him what had happened, then she phoned up the doctor. Both my dad and the doctor arrived more or less together. I was put straight to bed. By this time big blisters had appeared all over my face, and eyebrows and eyelashes singed off, where the black bars of the grate had burnt into my skin. The doctor said I would be scarred for life. For the next few weeks I had to have two large pieces of muslin soaked in ointment, one on each cheek. It was terrible. I couldn't eat properly, so I was fed on liquid food. This was because I had one large blister on the side of my mouth, it stayed there longer than any of the other blisters, and I had special orders from the doctor that this blister on no accounts must be bursted.

After staying in bed a few days, I got so lonely and bored that I was allowed to come out into the living room provided there were no draughts. And I remember one day when I was fed up, my mum and dad tried to cheer me up, something was said and I burst out laughing, therefore my blister burst. Underneath was new skin and as all the old skin gradually came off, the scars after a few months disappeared and my face became very smooth, but that did not last. Before long I was back at school.

74   *Chris.* I was always in the wars. One night my mother and father went out to a show and left me in the care of my uncle. I was outside in the street playing with my bike when I rode over a loose paving stone and went straight over the handlebars. I now have a scar for life on my knee. Incidentally I could never remember my right from my left, so mum told me to remember my scar was on my right knee, and I remember by it still.

75   *Brian.* Walking back to the room with a bottle in each hand. Dad butted in and said 'you do not really need it, do you.' 'Yes,' came a reply. I started to drink and when it was shaken by me it just exploded in my face. A big cry came from the gas and followed by a large session of crying. All that was hurt was my finger. Everybody was saying how lucky I was, but nobody put a plaster on my finger.

When I finally did tell my mum she said 'how did you do that?' Before I had time to answer, it was stuck under the cold tap and stinging like blazes. Some small pieces stuck in and had to be pulled with two pennies for the tweezers, because the others had broken.

76   *Valerie.* In this year (1956) my mother died. She had been very ill for quite a long time at odd times.

One night she felt very ill, so my father called for an ambulance. We had been in bed, but got up when we knew she was going into hospital. That night we couldn't sleep for worrying. A few days later, we were told that we had to stay school dinners. We didn't know why it was, but it was because my father and four older sisters were going to a funeral.

We didn't know that our mother had died, nobody had told us, not in our family anyway. The top of our road there was a family of busybodies, one girl of the same age as me. When I got to school I met her and she told me that my mother had died, I didn't even know before then.

77   *Roger.* At school during one of our take-it-easy, do-nothing lessons, it was decided by our rather weak-willed teacher that we were to make these sort of flat faces on sticks, peculiar things. They were made out of plain cardboard, the features being crayoned on after the head had been stuck to the handle.

As it happened, in the end, my face did not turn out very well. The person sitting next to me, however, did quite a good one. I suppose I must admit it—I was jealous. He showed the teacher his face-on-a-stick and was highly praised for it. The boy began to walk back to his seat, his face beaming. It was then that I had a most evil idea. As he was sitting down, I noticed that he had applied his wax crayon to the face very thickly and heavily.

My friend was a very gullible person. Taking advantage of this, I then proceeded to convince him that he would obtain a much better effect than he had if he scraped off the surplus wax with his finger-nails. He thought it was a marvellous idea and he immediately put the plan into practice.

When he had got half way down the head, he exclaimed that it was not turning out as I said it would. I reassured him by telling him that it looked far better when all of it had been scraped. So he continued scraping intently. At last he finished and let out a cry of dismay. The teacher sympathised with him, but the damage had been done. I sympathised with him too.

78   *John.* I was transferred to a fear-ruled school. Mr Jones was the name of the headmaster, he was an irritable old man who wore glasses and a bald head. His short form never prevented him from delivering his ultimate punishment, the cane. He would cane anyone for anything, and having caned, would move on to inflict more pain by cane.

The next step in my school ladder was Miss Green's class. Miss Green was a little old woman who had a thing about flying and the wheel's history. She was great fan of Old Fred who did the Nature Study broadcasts, we never missed him. Another pet subject of Miss Green's was R.I. She treated this subject with great care and gave the impression that she was seriously religious. We were forever drawing pictures of Moses, Amos, Abraham and other biblical greats.

79   *Suky.* He taught us first about the radius of circles and things like that. Then he went on about verbs, nouns, adverbs etc. When he began his lessons he would get out a bendy cane from his cupboard and stand in front of the class, bending it threateningly. Then he would proceed to walk round the class asking questions, and God help you if you did not know he would stand in front of you, stick out his stomach even more, his cheeks would bulge and he would bang on the desk with his cane.

80   *Raymond.* Our teacher was Mr Lock, he would tell us to close our eyes at the end of school and guess when one minute was up. If you guessed right you went out first amid the envy of the others.

81   *Eddie.* When we had finished we took the sums to be marked, making sure to stand well away from her desk so that she could not reach out and slap our legs, but if she wanted to

slap she would lure you towards the desk and say, 'What does that say?' and then lash out with her hand.

82   *Jack*. This is why I never took my book out the front to be marked. But one day she called me out and when she looked at it, she hit me with the ruler and sent me back to do the sums again. But I only copied off the person next to me and got hit again.

83   *Raymond*. The next term's prize was won by Alan Blakeley who got most of his points from sitting up straight.

84   *Laura*. The first holiday that came when I was at school was the half term. In the holidays it was cold and wet so mum bought me a pair of Wellingtons. The first day I had them I put them straight on and went out and strode through all the puddles, I was very proud of my boots and showed them off to everyone. That night I cleaned and dried them and took them to bed with me. The next day I put the boots on and went up the hill and at the top of the hill is a kind of wood and in there is a puddle about two feet deep. I didn't know that of course, so I stepped right in it. I managed to get out and went home wondering what mum would say.
    Then I had an idea. Outside our window was a rain butt, so I stood the Wellingtons on the window-sill just above the butt. Then I called my brother to open the window, when he did the boots fell off and into the water.

85   *Eunice*. Dan was a very lively boy and so he turned me into a real tomboy of which I was until 1960 when I became a bit more lady-like, but not much (I still aren't).
    When I got home three hours later (as I always went slow) I eagerly opened the present from her but it was a doll of

all things and for me. I cried I wanted a gun. 'Take it back,' I screamed, but I just had to put up with it, even though I've still got it now, never been used. My mum and dad bought me a cow-girl's outfit.

86   *Molly.* It was Easter when mum was still in hospital. I was recovered, but the doctor said, 'Be careful how you go about because you have a weak heart.'

Soon mum was home and well, I thought to myself many a time that I would be good, but I was born mischievous and so I would have to live with it all my life. It was Summer, I often went for walks along the roads or paths leading into some woods. One day I went on my own. I went in there and started to look into the pond where there lived fishes and frogs. Just behind the pond there were some stinging nettles, a bird behind me gave me a scare, so that I jumped and lost my balance and fell into the stinging nettles. I was lucky because the girl who was taking me out saw me fall and came running to me. I was screaming, because the spots looked like measles, but soon I calmed down after knowing that they were just ordinary spots.

87   *Annette.* My mum used to go to work before I left for school. One morning I went out into the garden to play with our dog (Peter) and I took the clock with us because I was afraid of being late, and I put the clock on the window sill. While I was playing with Peter I knocked the clock over and the glass was smashed. Being scared to tell my mum, I hid the glass and put the clock back indoors.

When I got home I hopefully looked at the clock, wishing that the glass was back in place. But I wished in vain. Later my mum and dad came home and I avoided all talk of the time. While I was up in my bedroom my mother had apparently noticed that the clock was broken, for when I came downstairs she said to me,

'Annette, do you know how the clock got broken?'

'No, mum,' I lied.

'Are you sure?' she asked.

'Yes,' again I lied.

But she seemed to realise that I was lying, for she said, ' If you dropped it own up and tell me. I won't be cross. But if you lie to me I will be cross. Did you or did you not drop the clock?'

' No, I didn't do it,' was my guilty reply.

But she knew I had done it, because she tried to put the wind up me by saying, ' Well, if you didn't do it we must have had burglars. I'll have to call the police.'

With that I was really frightened, so I blurted out,' Don't call a policeman, mum. I did it. I took it in the garden and knocked it off the window sill. I'm very sorry.'

'Just for telling lies you shan't have any sweets this week. It's not because you broke the clock, but because you lied,' replied my mum.

I went to my bedroom, sobbing, and hating my mother for inflicting such a terrible punishment on me. I laid on my bed and thought, 'I'll make you sorry, maybe I'll die and you'll all cry and wish you hadn't been so terrible to me.'

But unfortunately I didn't die and neither mum or dad seemed sorry that they had been so terrible to me; even when I refused to kiss my parents goodnight.

The next day when I went to school, my friend, Pat, offered me a sweet.

At home that evening I triumphantly announced to my mum,' Pat gave me a sweet today.' But she didn't seem to care, for all she said was, 'Oh! Did she?'

88   *Andrew.* It was round about this time that I had my first fag, we rode for miles jumped over streams and then started our fags. The boys I was with lighted my fag and I took my first drag. I was coughing and spluttering for five minutes, I also partly choked to death.

    I put the fag out and started a cigar. It was one of those big Churchill's cigars in a long tin tube, the cigar itself was about six inches long. I bit off the end and spat it away. I then put it in my mouth, the boy lighted it and I had a puff. You may have thought that I would have choked to death, but funnily I seemed to get on with it. But after I had finished I could hardly stand up. I was so dizzy that I fell flat on the ground.

89   *Sue.* My brothers would see me safely to Sunday School and then instead of them coming, they would go off to the brook (in their best clothes). There they would wade in the water and get soaking wet and filthy dirty. Other than getting wet and dirty they would go to my Uncle's and play billiards and my uncle never split on them until mum found out.

90   *Nicholas.* I wasn't really listening to the radio but two men were talking to each other and vaguely I heard one say that science and religion did not go hand in hand. I rather liked the sound of that phrase and had every intention of making full use of it.

    The next step was to break the news to my parents that I had made up my mind to become a scientist when I grew up and after repeating the phrase told them that it was no longer necessary to go to Sunday School.

91   *Helene.* My holidays are spent usually taking Shaun and Candy or my other sister's children, Douglas and Hilary out for walks or shopping. I am also trusted to give them their tea, bath

and put them to bed, which I often do if the mum is not home by a certain time.

Both Shaun and Candy enjoy an after-tea or a bedtime story and the ones they like best are about dogs or some kind of animals, including the Three Bears, with all the voices added for daddy bear, mummy bear and baby bear and I get told if the voices do not go with the character concerned. If I give baby bear a big deep voice or daddy bear a tiny squeaky voice, I get told off and have to start again.

If I tell them a story of poor dolly who broke her arm, I get told, 'No, she's got chippin pox or the flu not poor arm.'

92   *Angela*. We are the only ones in the family really alike one another. We always agreed with each other about things. Although she is four years older than me I always told her when Dave (her boy friend) would like the way she dressed best. I was nearly always right. We always (or at least I did) tried to look alike. When she got a new dress I would buy material to make a dress the same as hers.

As she is a different religion to Dave, they had to get married in a registry office. Therefore none of us children could go to her wedding. The last time we saw her was before the wedding when she stepped into the car to take her to Southcliff.

Nobody took any notice of me after Molly got married, nobody agreed (or seemed to) about the things I spoke of, nobody even wore things like me. I felt lost as if I didn't know anyone at all.

93   *Chris*. My mum says one night I went up to her when she was knitting, and said 'Can you teach me to knit?' Mum says she will never forget it, as it was worse than teaching a cat to crochet. I am not much better now really.

94   *Lynne.* It was in the summer holidays when the sun burnt your skin that my friend Carol and I found we had nothing to do. Firstly we decided to be kind to our fathers. We got Carol's father his Sunday paper and polished his shoes, but when we asked if he would take us down the beach, the answer was no. The same happened when we asked my dad, but he only said if we wanted something to do we should help him with the garden.

We were thinking of all those lucky people on the beach when I had a brainwave, it was watching dad water the garden; why shouldn't we have an ice cold shower under the hose. I asked and dad said it was all right.

Carol got her swimsuit and I got mine. We put them on and went into the garden where we found the sun was hot on our backs. Alan was already out there. The hose was full on and when we got sprayed a horrible cold shiver went down my back. It wasn't a pleasant feeling—much too cold.

I tried not to get sprayed too much and when the sun went behind a cloud I started shivering and goose pimples arrived on my arms. So we went indoors leaving puddles of water all over the floor which made the grass stick to the floor.

95   *Susie.* When I was about eight years old, my mother as usual asked me to go down the shops to get some ham for my father's lunch the following morning, so I went down there with my younger sister. We got the ham and on the way back, my sister asked for a bit. I said no, for I knew if it was missed when I got home I should get the blame, She was silent for a little while and then she started moaning again and kept on saying, 'Go on only, only one tiny bit, one tiny weeny piece, only one mingy bit,' all the way up the road, she said this continuously. So in the end I gave in, anything for peace, so I gave her a bit; she wasn't satisfied until I gave her another. While she was eating this, it made me hungry, so I took a piece; while I was doing this she

accused me of taking too much, so I had to give her a bit more. In the end you can imagine how much was left.

We walked a little more and I was scared of the thought of what my mum was going to say. I wrapped the remainders up in my pocket, I went in the back door and laid the small package on the table and called,' Mum, I'm home,' and crept quietly out through the door.

Mum looked at the ham which was screwed up in little pieces and said, 'What on earth is this?' Have you been eating it?'

'No, mum.'

'Don't tell me she gave it you like this, well you can go back to the shop and tell her she didn't give you the correct amount.'

So I had to own up. My mum told me off at first, but later on she laughed and said, 'you're just as bad as your father.'

96   *Roger.* I was as yet not old enough to ride the sort of cycle he had. A Lenton racer with dropped handlebars that were covered in bright red tape. It wasn't a very marvellous bike, I realise now, but it looked wonderful to me at the time. My brother often used to come into the house, his face bright red and laced with sweat and foaming at the mouth. He then used to tell us how fast he had ridden. It was often up in the 4o's.

Whenever he used to tell us all of his feats, I used to watch the expression on my mother's face, it was an expression of inner pain and torture for I knew that she hated to know how fast he had been. All she could do was to wait until the day he would gain one mile an hour too many and crash.

97   *Raymond.* On Empire Day everybody came to school dressed up as cowboys, cubs, brownies or wore their best clothes. I was too young to understand what Empire Day was, so I went as usual. At assembly the people who were dressed up

were told to step up on the platform. Someone behind me put up their hand and said, 'I've got my best suit on.' They were told to go up on the platform, so I put up my hand and said, 'I've got my best tie on.' To this everybody laughed, I did not know why, so I looked round bewildered. But I was called up on the platform.

98   *Angela*. At Christmas all the children would sit in the hall around the big Christmas tree and sing Christmas carols. Then an important person would come up to us in turn and give us a present; whilst doing so she would shake our hand. I can remember having asked if she had a present on the tree and said thank you for the toy. She said 'no' and carried on giving the other children their presents.

I asked my teacher who was standing near me if I could get something out of my desk. I went and got a pencil, then went and sat on the floor again, only this time near the tree. Before this important woman went to get another present off the tree, I put the pencil on the branch of the tree. The woman picked it up and asked whose it was and I told her it was hers, because she didn't have one.

All the teachers laughed at this, but as I looked one by one at them, they stopped. The woman said she wouldn't forget me for giving it to her and I bet she doesn't.

99   *Jeannette*. On a Wednesday afternoon we would have the radio on, we would dance and sing to the music. All the girls had a boy partner. My partner's name was Alan. He kept treading on my toes or he would fall over and drag me over or he would skip so fast that I would fall over and the teacher would remind Alan the tune didn't go that fast.

There was a teacher I had that used to pull your teeth out if they were loose.

100   *John.* When we had a school play, 'The Sleeping Beauty', I was a duck, a chicken or some other beaked fowl, and although I was not allowed to wear my cowboy chaps, I enjoyed the rehearsals.

In a later Christmas nativity play, I was a peasant who said 'not very far' to the question 'How far is it to Bethlehem?'

101   *Janice.* Our class was doing a little play that I can't remember much about, I suppose that is because I wasn't in it. But I was in the choir and the band. I played a tambourine, although I always wanted to play the drums and cymbals, but I never did; those parts went to the teacher's pets.

The play went on first, and we had to stand in the wings. Well, it wasn't really the wings, it was just a curtain which had been hung from the ceiling. You see we didn't have a proper stage we had to hire a sort of portable one. Anyway the play went off all right; one girl forgot her lines and Miss Johns was almost shouting herself silly, trying to make her hear.

Then it was our turn, the curtains were closed as we climbed onto the stage. We left our tambourines, triangles etc at the back of the stage and went to form our four rows with Miss Ward standing in front of us to conduct.

I knew there was only the rest of the school watching, but I was still nervous. And as the curtains opened I felt glad that I was in the second row and not in the first. I remember moving along a little, so that I was hidden by the girl in front of me. We sang three songs and everybody clapped.

102   *Robert.* One day when I was about eight years old I went to visit a house in London on a Saturday morning.

'We came to look over the house,' my mother said to the woman.

We first went upstairs to look in the bedrooms. There was one very small room and it had not got any cupboard. It was painted with a dark green which I said I did not like, so we went into the other one. This was a big one and was painted a bright yellow and in it were some cupboards. These I tried to pull open, but I could not because they were locked. I unlocked the cupboard and pulled open the door and inside was a small box. I pulled it out and lifted the flap and inside was a tortoise. It must have been left there by the other people.

I took it out and put it on my hand. It put his head out and looked round to see what was happening. It tried to walk on my hand, but could not.

I pulled another cupboard open and in it was a box of straw, when the tortoise saw this he tried to get into it. I helped him to get into the box of straw and shut the flap down and put him back in the cupboard and locked the doors.

103   *John*. When I was eight I had my first ride on a horse. I rode it quite successfully, but when I dismounted, the docile little beast stamped on my foot and that forever leaves me with a wariness of horses, particularly the rear end.

104   *Lawrence*. My mum, my brother and I went to Southcliff, when we came back we found that my dad had the floorboards up to rescue a baby sparrow. It had fallen out of the nest in the ventilator upstairs and fallen between the walls and ended up underneath the floor.

My dad had heard him cheeping. When he found out that he was there he had the floorboards up. Then he had the job to get the bird to come to the opening in the floor within reach. He put some bread down and eventually it struggled there. It could not fly at all and it could barely walk. We had to keep it for just over a week and when it was well again, we took a photograph of it on my shoulder. The shutter clicked and then he flapped his wings and flew away.

105   *Marilyn.* Mice, we had a lot of those, so to get rid of them we had a lot of cats. I remember one cat in particular, a large black one that was more hair than cat. His tail was long and he carried it upright. His body was roundish with hair standing on end and his ears were only just showing through the vast covering mass of hair.

When he ever caught a mouse the poor thing would be dropped on the back doorstep and the cat would sit watching it, checking every move it made by a swipe of his paw.

106   *Eunice.* On this weekend that Anne came to stay we had a new cat and my sister's dog Trixie chased it. So my sister had her dog put to sleep. I cried bitterly for I loved it more than the cat.

107   *Doreen.* I had a surprise when I returned home from school, for mum and dad had bought two dozen chicks to keep in our chicken shed when they were old enough. The chicks were soft and fluffy and very delicate and one chick in particular was weaker than the rest and looked after by mum.

A couple of days later the chick was in a critical state and to try and revive it mum gave it a teaspoonful of brandy that was kept for medical purposes. The chick then felt cold and so it was placed in the oven at a low number and in a few hours was as strong and as full of life as any of the others.

108   *Annette.* I have always been fond of animals; although I did, one day, paint our dog (Peter) from head to tail with varnish which my mum had left on the table, while she went to answer the door.

Apart from liking animals I never had any fear of them, and at the age of three I used to sit under the milkman's horse and cuddle his legs.

109   *Roger.* I remember going for long walks with my father and our dog. What a wonderful dog he was. I will never forget the day we had to have him destroyed.

On Thursday, the twelfth of February, he became terribly ill with a heart attack. I remember lying on my bed, shaking and crying, I knew what was to follow.

On Friday the thirteenth of February he had to be destroyed. I left the house for four hours whilst the vet was there. I had never felt so miserable before. What year all this took place, I don't know.

110   *Lucy.* One day I was riding up a hill just for the ride, it was a very steep one and I used to ride down at top speed. I was on my way up when a man came and said,' Come over here a minute,' so I did. He said, 'Where is Latton Bush?' I told him. He asked, 'What's your name pretty girl, and where do you live?' being a stupid nit I told him. After, he asked would I like to come for a ride in the car. I said 'no' and that I had my own bike to ride on, and with that I rode off.

I noticed he was behind me in the car, so I raced back home and I went speeding down the hill with him just behind my tail, so I went faster. I slammed on the brakes when I went round the corner, he went the opposite way. By this time I parked my bike outside and rushed into the house and told my mum. She didn't believe me at first, but when she saw my hands, she saw they were shaking like a leaf. So she rushed for the phone box and called for the police. And they were here in a few ticks and they asked me a lot of questions.

After that a few months later I saw him again, but after that I didn't see him again, after that I didn't see him any more.

111   *Jacqueline.* I heard a scream. It was Rosemary. I cried out, 'What's wrong?'

She replied, 'There's a face at the back door.'

I said, 'Don't be silly.' She said, 'I am not.'

I thought I am not having this, so I went out to the kitchen, sure enough there was a face outside the door.

I suggested we turn the light out and get a couple of saucepans, then hide under the table and wait. Then all of a sudden the doorknob turned slowly and then gradually the door opened and who should walk in but Rosemary's mum. She walked over to the light and turned it on, 'What do you think you're doing?'

112   *Angela.* As I was going on holiday, I thought I'd polish up on some dancing, so I started doing the waltz on my own when I felt a terrifying tap on my shoulder. But when I turned round there wasn't anyone in sight, so I ran into the end part of the room where the settee was. I jumped onto it.

I held my breath. I must have been standing there for quarter of an hour. I kept saying to myself I wasn't going to worry, but I couldn't get over the thought of nobody being around when I could have sworn somebody had tapped me on the shoulder. I couldn't move and I couldn't breathe, every noise like that of rose bushes moving, and that of deep breathing from Roger and Peter and the dog made me even more scared.

113   *Christina.* Mum's bedroom was being decorated and they were sleeping in the front room. I didn't like this bed room very much because it was a rather large room with a dark oak dressing table with tallboy and wardrobe to match. The wardrobe was

very solemn and dark. The bed was a large double bed with a springy mattress. The wallpaper was blue and pink diamonds made of little flowers. Once I had slept in it and didn't enjoy it.

The light in the bedroom had been taken out and put in my brother's bedroom for the moment and it was all in the dark except for the lamp outside the window which shone through the lace curtains and gave the feeling as though you weren't alone in the room. Every now and again the bed would shake violently. It was most probably the springs, but it rather scared me. The tall dark wardrobe in the corner reminded me of when I was small and I went to see Southcliff lights. On a small hill was Ghostland and one thing I have never forgotten is the Ghosts that lived in a tall dark wardrobe came out all covered in a kind of cobweb, coloured misty-green mauve, red.

114   *Laura.* That night every time I closed my eyes I could see that man. Outside it was raining but I didn't know. When I heard the noise that rain makes on the roof, I thought that it was the monster climbing over the roof and was going to get in through the window. The rain came in the window and splashed on my face. I thought the monster had got into my room and that it was the blood from his face dripping onto mine. Then a wind blew up and the board that covers the hole to the loft shifted. That was all I could stand, so I let out a scream and began to cry. Before I knew where I was I was being carried into my parents' room by my dad and I snuggled up to my mum. Just before I went to sleep I heard her say,' She won't look at another film like that for a long time now.'

115   *Christina.* After I had moved back into my bedroom I shut Dad's bedroom door because from my bed I could see into their bedroom. Next morning the door was open. Mum and dad were not sleeping there, so I shut it again. Then the next night I

jammed it tight with a sock in, but again the next morning it was open. I was positive that there were ghosts in the house or equally as odd and again the next night I jammed it closed with three socks, so even when I tried to open it, it wouldn't. But then again the next morning the socks were lying on the floor.

116   *Elizabeth*. One day my sister and her friend Sheila came home with two long green sticks, my sister Ann, Pat and myself asked them what they were. They told us that an old lady in a caravan had given them to them and that they were magic. They told us that they could turn us into anything they wanted to. Thelma my sister said that she could turn me into a spider. At which I said, 'Go on, then.' To cover up for herself she said, 'Well I can't turn you back again and I'll stamp on you and kill you.' At this I ran into the house and told dad. He took the sticks away from them and broke them.

117   *Johnny*. Outside the pictures there was a mound on which we played for a few minutes. And afterwards by cutting through somebody's garden we arrived at the High Street. Here we bought sixpennyworth of chips which we took on a bus bound for home. When we had eaten all our chips we got to the window, screwed the greasy chip paper in a ball and chucked it out, hoping it would hit somebody on the head. When we came to our bus stop we got off, had a bit of fun around the petrol pumps and then headed home.

118   *Geoffrey*. A grumpy old man came round ushering everyone off. No sooner had he gone when everybody came back. Another five minutes later and he came back with a watering can. Naturally we thought he was going to water the plants, but to our dismay he told everyone to move and then he

watered the wall on which we had been sitting on, so that we could no longer sit there.

119   *Sally*. The builders started to dig up the fields at the back of us. We used to go over there to play, but one day Mark, Raymond and my brother were playing over there when they found a bomb but they didn't know this at the time.

They brought it into our back garden to show my dad, he came out and called Mr Williams, he came quickly and they said it was a German bomb. So all us kids went to the police station. We knocked at the door, but no one answered. After knocking louder, a policeman came to the door in his braces. We told him about the bomb. He didn't believe us. He gave us the benefit of the doubt and said he would be along in about five minutes.

He parked his car on the new road which was being built and came over to where the bomb was. He asked who found it; he then asked whereabouts we found it. Mark answered, 'Just near where your car is.' And you should have seen the policeman's face.

120   *Christopher*. One Saturday we were out playing when we saw some boys playing by the pond which is now covered by the school field. When we got near them we saw that they were throwing pieces of cotton with fat worms on them into the water, then they counted up to a hundred. After they had finished counting they all pulled up their lines and to our amazement every one of them had a great fat wriggly four-legged water lizard on the end, or so we thought; but we later found out that they were king newts, teeming in the pond.

121   *Suky*. I went to Guides every Thursday and had good fun. In Summer we went on sort of hunts. We were given a list of things which we had to find, like a horse's hair which we

pulled out of a passing dog, a match box which we usually found in a rubbish bin, also a ladybird to go in it. We usually found them in the midst of stinging nettles and we often got stung trying to get one.

122   *Mary*. One day our friend George, David and I went up to an old empty cottage. We decided to play at being pirates. We were at the top window of the cottage, (about fifteen feet up), when in our game the ship was sinking. George, the captain, yelled, 'Every man for himself!'

David, misunderstanding his meaning, jumped straight out of the window onto the grass below.

He landed with a thud and lay still. George looked at me and I looked at him. For a moment we just stood there, and then we made a frantic rush for the stairs. We got to David who was still lying there. George tentatively shook him and David said, ' Shut up I'm in Davy Jones' Locker.'

123   *Graham*. At playtime about eight of us would lock arms round each other's necks and go round the playground shouting, 'Cowboys and Indians', so that we could get enough to have a game; but by the time we had persuaded half of the boys to have a game the bell would go and we would have to line up.

I remember some of the children would stand in the lines all playtime, so that they could be first into school. During the dinner hour we would have time to have a good game of 'Cowboys and Indians' and we would fight to see which side won. I was always the leader of the Cowboys and my friend Brian would be the leader of The Indians.

124   *Royston*. I looked around to see if there was anybody I could play with, I saw another boy standing on his own and went over to talk to him. His name was Paul Barnes and he always

wore a black raincoat and a black blazer. He was rather fat like someone in our class.

I always knew where to find him in the mornings because he would always stand by Mr Jones's railings. At different times of the day you could find him in different places. In the mornings he would be by the railings, at morning break he would be by the huts and at dinner time he would be by the field.

125   *Mick*. By now the conker season was in and I was very pleased and so we went up to a man's house. He was an ex-army officer and his name was Mr. Drake and he was a sly old chap. We went to get some conkers and in the getting — lots of things happened because when we were getting in a big dog came up and so we climbed up the nearest tree and it was a horse chestnut. So we got the chestnuts and threw them down at the dog and hit it on its nose. It gave a grave yelp and ran away, tail between its legs, and so we carried on getting the chestnuts.

This man, Mr. Drake had a son about eleven and we were only about eight or nine, then when he came over we hit him and he began to cry. So he went and got his dad. He came, so we climbed up the tree again. We held our breath and then he looked about and saw us up the tree. So the man called us to come down and when we got down he sent a letter to the head at our school. The next morning in assembly my friends' names and mine were read out and we had to see him.

Everybody was very tense waiting outside his office. He called us in one by one and then he asked us why we went that way home and he said ' if I get any more complaints about you you will get the cane.'

That night we went to get some more conkers and then we climbed up the tree and as we were leaving he caught us again. And so it got back to the headmaster and in assembly he called our names out again and we waited outside his office very tense and then he said 'come in' and he went over to the corner and there was a bamboo cane and it tapers down to a tiny point and then said 'hold out your hand' and so I held my hand out and as the cane came down I moved my hand and he said ' for that I will give you three strokes' and so he gave me them. Then I chased downstairs to the toilets and put my hand in cold water and that felt much better and most of my friends came down crying and so we went back to class.

126   *Suzanna.* Us four always sat in the front upstairs and if there were little children they were told to be obedient and get out. We, as you can imagine, got rather bored having two hours' travelling each day.

So we made things to do, such as collected bus tickets (lucky ones also, which numbers added to twenty one). We had penny bubble gum contests to see who could make the biggest bubble. Johanna was the champion. Also on the number one bus we were the catscradle champions. The first French I learnt on a bus was from Barbara and Janet who both learnt French. We didn't get far, but I think in about three weeks we learnt the numbers.

On the way back the bus was always full, so Jo, Me, Rhubarb (Barbara) and Janet used to annoy people and also there were five fat boys from another school who used to catch our bus in the evening. We used to fight and I used to scratch and bite and come home filthy. If a conductor came upstairs, Janet who was the nicest talker would put on her best face and offer him a sweet, and if that didn't work nothing would.

127   *Pamela.* It was nearly half past ten and the boy next door who was two years and one day older than me asked if he could come round and play until dinner time. I went in and asked my mum and she said he could. He said he would get on his horse

and be right over. I was quite surprised to think he was coming on a horse. When he strolled round the corner of the house I said to him: 'Well, where is your horse?'

And he said ' I haven't got off of it yet.'

'Oh!' I said.

'You didn't think it was a real one did you?' he said.

'Oh no,' I replied.

128   *Johnny.* One time my parents bought me a tool kit, but I suppose I can't really call it this, because all it consisted of was a saw, a hammer and a screwdriver. I was also given a piece of wood and some nails. When I was given these I thought I would knock a few nails into the provided wood. I knew how to do it because I had seen my father do it several times. I held the nail in my left hand and with the hammer in my right I struck away at the nail. Directly the hammer touched the nail or should I say my finger, the nail shot across the other side of the lean-to, taking with it a piece of skin. I tried again, but this time instead of holding the nail in my fingers when I hit it, I would let go before the hammer touched it and as a result would still have a complete finger left.

Down swung the hammer, away came my fingers, bang went the hammer as it met the wood, but instead of the nail being knocked into the wood it was lying on the mat. Several times I tried this, but I made no progress.

At last my father tapped the nail into the piece of wood leaving me at least three quarters left to hit. Once again down came the hammer making a ringing sound. I then brought away the hammer expecting the nail to be pounded into the wood, but instead it was bent into several shapes. Getting a bit wild I gave it up as a bad job.

129   *Christopher.* On firework night we were watching a big 2/6d rocket come up from the ground in a large arc and come down again. At that moment the rocket finished it sped to earth through heaps of darkness. Just at that moment my dad held the back of his neck. The stars had fallen down his neck, the rocket was lying on the ground near the fire. By this time the guy was just a smouldering heap of rubble, his head was hanging over the side of the old arm chair we had sat him on. Next to the chair was a flat piece of tin with the dud fireworks on it.

Just at that moment a jumping jack goes off, a person screams, then the sound dies down for the jack has come to the end of its jumping path. After this someone let a 'helicopter' off, it buzzes over the fence into the next door garden. It spun on the ground, scorching the grass. It spurts out a small shower of sparks, then it died down.

People were going inside for hot cocoa and to let the cats and dogs out from the cupboard under the stairs.

130   *Alan.* By West Kensington railway station there was a very big debris and a number of bombed but still standing houses in which no one lived, this debris had a very big sewer running underneath it. This sewer was very clean because for some reason it had never been used. The entrance to the sewer was a hatch-cover over a hole.

The hole had a ladder running down the side of it. The ends of the sewer had been filled in. So, being daring as most of my friends were we all went down into the sewer. Down the sewer it was cold and dark so most of my friends would not go down for fear of a so-called bogyman, which we all thought lived in a black hole in the ground and gobbled up any little boys or girls playing out in the dark. But instead of us going down in the dark of the sewer (because the sewer was so deep, although being three o'clock in the afternoon it was not any lighter inside) we all got as many torches, candles and matches as we could find for we decided to explore the sewer under candle and torchlight.

After some time, because the wind kept blowing them out, we managed to light one candle and a boy, David his name was, he was ten years old, went down the ladder first with the candle. We all, except one boy, who was staying at the top as a look-out, went down into the sewer. We sat upon a kind of ledge and stood the candles up in a line in front of us and lit them from the other candle. This made the sewer a bit lighter so we started to explore.

About an hour later two of the candles had gone out. Because we had so many candles alight, it began to get stuffy in the sewer and it was quite warm too. So we all got out of the sewer and sat at the top of the hole. We sat there some time, thinking how we could turn the sewer into a sort of hide-out. So, after deciding what to do, we all went home to have a late dinner.

After our dinner we returned bringing as many bits of wood, nails and other bits and pieces (such as string and if possible a hammer) as we could find. We all met at the top of the hole and sorted out the bits and pieces we had. Among what was brought we had an oil drum, which the look-out beat with a stick when anyone was coming, the bottom of an old oil stove which we put oil into after finding some left in the oil drum, about eight sacks, an old table cloth and two very large bed sheets and half of a mattress.

We decided to hide the entrance of the sewer, so with a spade which one boy brought we dug up earth and piled it round the hole and put clumps of grass on the earth. The bump, that was what it looked like when we had finished was like any other bump on the bomb site.

All the bits and pieces we thought would come in handy we threw down the sewer. We then started to build down the sewer a kind of underground hut. This turned out quite well, as it was big enough for all of us to get in without being crowded together.

Whenever we left the sewer someone always had to stand guard above the hole, but with the bits of string we had, to stop anyone going down and giving the secret of our hideout away, we made booby traps, such as string across the ladder, so that when someone trod on it, it would shake a string of tin cans and they would probably be frightened because as it was dark they would not know what it was.

We tried this out on the boy who acted as look-out, being above, he would not know what we were doing. We all got out of the sewer and told the boy to go into the sewer and fetch a spanner. He went down the steps until he was out of sight, for the ladder went down a long way and the string was tied about half-way down it. We heard the echo of the tin cans and the boy came running back up the ladder.

' There's a bogyman down there and it tried to get me!' he shouted.

About two months later one morning we were all going to the sewer when we saw that the site had been fenced off and houses were being built on part of the site. At night, when the workmen had all gone home, we crept into the site and to our surprise found that the sewer entrance had been cemented up.

131   *Jim.* Within a week I knew most of the kids in the neighbourhood, but there was a regular bunch of five. This vast crowd of people called itself a gang and appointed me as their leader. Our gang consisted of a fat boy—a very fat boy who had to have special trousers made for his carcase. Another member of the gang was a smaller boy not only in build but in general size. Maybe he was small but he was tough, he could smash a brick wall down with his head and not know it. Paul was the thin one and was a bit of a cry baby and was always sulking.

One weekend when me and the gang were playing around the pond, which is a dismal thing at the best of times, we met the disaster which was to come to Roynton. The disaster was a boy of about nine years old, his name was Richard Myers. When I met him he was playing at the edge of our pond. I wished he could have drowned that day, it certainly would have saved me some trouble. You see a few weeks later he moved on to our estate. Richard Myers soon got up a rival gang.

We often had battles with each other. I liked the street battles. My gang got behind Paul's (the second in command) garden wall. The walls were not very high and we could kneel on the ground and still look over the top. When each gang was dug in the artillery would proceed to open fire. The artillery consisting of boys with lumps of dried mud or stones. The amazing thing is that nobody got hurt, at least nobody on our side. The mud bombs were best, we all used to like to see them hit the enemies' wall and ricochet off.

There was one boy at Roynton who was just like a little Hitler or a Mussolini. One day during a school holiday somehow an argument started between my gang and this boy, who I will call Hitler. We started to make a den in Johnny's garden and Hitler made his out of a pile of bricks left by some workmen. Every now and then one of us would creep along and spy on Hitler. If one of the gang was caught by him, he was much bigger than us. Well if he caught us he would make us work on his castle. We had to call him sir and if we refused which we did, he would hit us across the face. When it was Tubby's turn to spy on the enemy, he was captured as he was too fat to dodge between brick piles.

132   *Ken.* The mob was called up and it was divided into two almost equal parts one side of course being the Germans and the other the British. Whenever playing wars I always wanted to be

on the German side because I loved to do my spectacular dying leaps, and of course since the British were never killed the Germans it had to be.

At the top of our road there was a main road with a large park across the other side. This park was known as the chase and was private, but knowing that the only guard was half blind and never left his hut it was quite safe to play there.

I immediately decided (being leader of the Germans of course) that we would withdraw into the woods in the chase hence, leading the British into a most cunning and dastardly ambush which I had previously arranged with the Martin brothers who would do anything for a penny lollipop, providing they were raspberry flavoured.

We withdrew into the clearing where the ambush was to take place, when suddenly one of my men let loose a counter attack! But it was too late! Whilst Randle's only man held them off for a few seconds with a continuous stream of wasted cap smoke, Randle had plastered Uncle Fred's car with mud thrown at a distance.

'You're blown up,' he was yelling triumphantly. 'You're both blown up and dead.' ' Hmm,' I thought a blazing tank wouldn't do without any smoke. So I searched for a box of matches in the glove compartment and lit an old A.A. map on the floor of the car. It was smoking nicely when Derek Martin came roaring round the block corner on my brother's late 300 c.c. 'Your brother's been nabbed for speeding, he's up by the co-op,' he yelled. With this in mind, the whole mob sped off towards the High Street, completely forgetting the blazing 'tank'. When I came back on the pillion of my brother's motor bike, I found that a neighbour had put it out and except for a pile of ashes on a rubber mat which looked like it had gone back to its natural state, the light brown upholstered front seat had now gone dark brown and black in some places and this was the extent of the damage.

133   *Christina.* It was Saturday when a friend of mine called Gillian came down for the day. We had just eaten dinner and had got nothing to do, so I suggested going down to the river which was only a little way down the road. So, putting our rubber boots on, we marched off down to the river. After splashing about in the water, we started walking about in the mud—popping sea weed. We went further and further out, the mud suddenly became very sticky and deep! Gillian became stuck, so I went over to help her out, but in doing so I became stuck.

At last I managed to loosen myself and then get free; the mud by this time was level with the rubber boot or Wellington boot as most people call them, so Gillian could not get out. Staggering across to her, my feet feeling as if they weighed half a ton with all the mud clinging to them. I could get Gillian free, but without my mother's boots. As we were pulling hard she overbalanced and had to put her foot down in the mud, which just came below her knee. Not making matters any better, she had long white socks on. When I tried to move I found I was stuck just as much as Gillian. Again leaning forward to try and pull Gillian out I realised that she was too far away and so I went headlong into the mud.

After some time a few boys came along and laughed at us. They asked if we were stuck and just trying to be funny I said 'No', so the boys just went away.

134   *Jean.* Nearly every year we went away for our holidays, but for the past three years we hadn't done so. Then we decided to go to Devon. We arranged to go in the afternoon as soon as I had come home from school at dinner-time. After dinner I said goodbye to my friends and walked out of school. The rain that

had been threatening to come down made a final burst and came down heavily.

As I stood by the bus-stop I got soaked since I had only plimsolls on and no coat. I waited there for ten minutes, but the bus didn't come, so I started running. When I was half-way down the hill, the bus passed me, spraying me with mud. That was the limit; with tears streaming down my face, I started running again. I soon got the stitch. I sheltered in a doorway for five minutes, with the rain pouring down and lightning and thunder beginning.

I had to get home by half past two and it was already ten past, so I started running again, getting splashed every two minutes by passing cars. When I got to the 'Village' I had another rest, but I had to get on—the time was quarter past. Just then as I was crossing a road I had to pull up sharp. By the side of the road a stream was gaily running. It was about three feet wide and didn't finish until the road branched off, so I had to take a running jump and hope for the best. I nearly did it, but I stumbled and my feet got soaking wet. The passers by gave me sympathetic smiles and hurried on.

The time had just gone twenty past as I reached the caravan site. The bridge was flooded and a car had got stuck, it was being pulled to one side so that other cars could get through. I edged myself through the crowd that still gathered even if it was raining. I ran till I couldn't run any more. I walked till I got my breath back. Another bus passed.

'I'll never get there in time,' I thought, sobbing between my breaths. The thunder and lightning was getting worse. As I turned the corner I bumped into Mrs Jameson coming out of a house.

'My dear, you're soaking wet!' she said.

'Please let me go. I have to be home by half past two,' I asked. ' I'll take you in the car, then,' she said, bustling me in.

135   *David.* The train journey was one of the longest I can remember. The train had tables in it and was packed full. It was a very hot day and for most of the journey the sun was glaring in through the grimy train window. For some of the time we played cards or read comics that mum had bought, back at the nameless station.

Most of the passengers in that carriage were very hot and didn't try to hide the fact. One man near me was reading a paper. He was reading the back page with the sport on it, so I had to be content with reading the front. It wasn't very interesting. I was glad when he turned the paper around so that I could read the football results.

Even they didn't seem very interesting, so I read the account of how, the week before, a man had won thousands of pounds on the pools. There was a picture of him holding up an illegible cheque. The top half of his head was chopped off, just showing his triumphant grin.

Then I was bored again so I started to draw funny men on the dusty window on my left, but mum told me to stop because I was getting my finger dirty. Anyway I ran out of dirt.

136   *Roger.* I can remember well lying awake in our chalet, listening to the sea against the sea wall.   First a roll like thunder, then a gentle splashy patter in contrast as the spray hit the road.

137   *Sally.* There were 46 girls in our dormitory, so you can imagine what fun we had. The first and the last nights were the best. In the first night we all went to bed, but wouldn't stop talking; one girl was mucking about and put her hand through the window. That night we didn't get to sleep till about 11.30 and then I decided I wanted to go to the toilet, but it was right over the other side of the field. I asked if anyone else wanted to come

and only one girl wanted to. So we went up to the little room where the ladies in charge slept. I knocked on the door to ask if we could go (the other girl was hiding behind me). The woman said if we went everyone else would want to go. But after a bit of persuasion she said 'yes'. Well, when the other girls heard this they all wanted to go. We all rushed to the door and only the first ten were allowed to go. As we walked across the field some torches flashed on us, so we all started screaming and ran.

138 *Angela.* The first day on holiday (the first full day) we went for a walk in the town. It was smashing. There was:
1. The one-armed bandits and roundabouts;
2. Fish and chip shop;
3. Different toy and antique shops (things were nice and cheap);
4. Bingo;
5. Clothes shops, nothing over-expensive;
6. Best of all, ice cream stands and sweet shops, along with all different film star photos.

I can't remember everything that happened, but best of all there was Wilf, a lifeguard who worked in the swim-pool. 'Lifeguard' sounds good doesn't it? He was good-looking. Then there was Dennis, he was the Bingo man. He worked in the club; he too was good-looking. There was Derek who worked in a sweet shop and Mary, a girl who worked with Derek (she was Japanese). And Tony was the man who played the drums. He was very friendly, because he liked my family a lot; he was always playing the Cha cha, waltz, Twist, plus other dancing tunes. He played loud and quiet tunes, quick and slow dance tunes.

After doing some dancing my sister and I went into the Bingo room where Dennis would lift up his arm and wave a finger, it would mean we were to sit down and start playing.

Every now and again he would say: ' I'm losing my hair,' and 'my beer's bubbling over.'

139   *David.* There was a camp photographer who stood about in the camp centre taking snaps of people as they walked by. I had a contest with my sister to see who could get photographed the most times. I won. He took nine of me and five of my sister. Two of mine and two of my sister's both had us in together.

Every time he took a picture of you he gave you a ticket with a number on it. At the end of your holiday you took it to the camp shop where they showed you the photo and asked if you wanted to buy it or not. I thought dad was going to buy the lot, but he didn't. This made me very disappointed. Dad did in fact only buy one of them. He said this was the only good one. I always said afterwards that the only reason he bought it was because it was the only one with him in.

140   *June.* Now I must mention this funny incident which happened to Daddy. After the cup of tea, Mummy, Ricky and I got back in the car ready to move on, I must add it was still a slight drizzle, so we left Daddy to wind up the jacks on the caravan and lock the door.

Daddy found the toilet compartment window open, so he went into the toilet to shut it. On doing so the catch slipped down and locked him in, the window being a small one, Daddy was unable to climb out. Suddenly Mummy and I felt the car moving up and down, but did not take much notice as we thought Daddy was testing the springs or something. After about fifteen minutes we started to wonder what could be keeping Daddy so long. Mummy was just about to get out of the car when a lady knocked on the window and with a laugh said, 'I think your husband is locked in the toilet.' At this remark, Mummy got out of the car, splitting her sides with laughter, releasing an exhausted Daddy who had been jumping up and down for the last quarter of an hour trying to attract our attention. Mummy says she would have gone to investigate sooner, had it not been raining.

We reached Loch Ness without any more mishaps; for 32 miles my head was in one direction, looking towards Loch Ness for the monster.

141   *Paul.* Another memorable incident was when dad stopped the car on a small hill to go in a shop. Mum and I were sitting in the car talking when I noticed a lamp post overtaking us on the inside. Mum dived forward and yanked on the handbrake; dad came out of the shop and instead of finding the car standing in front of the shop, he found it parked 150 yards farther down the road.

The thing we enjoyed about the holiday most was not the distance we covered, because it took us hours to get anywhere, let alone get back; no, the thing we enjoyed was all the fresh air we got pushing it up hills.

142   *Linda.* My Granddad had decided to hire one of those three-wheeled bicycles which you find at most holiday camps. But my Granddad had to do all the pedalling as I could not reach the pedals.

When we reached the place where the flights left I was trembling. Granddad asked me if I still wanted to go and I bravely said 'yes'. So he went and bought the tickets. We had to wait for a few minutes as someone was already in one of the planes.

Our turn came and I climbed in. Granddad had to sit in the front so that he could help to balance the plane. The engine started and we sped along the long grass field. Then we were airborne. By this time I was enjoying it and when you looked out of the window the people looked like midgets. I didn't like going over the sea. It felt as though the plane had stopped and I felt I wanted to get out and push it.

After we had been up for about seven minutes, we started losing height. The field gradually came up to meet us. Then with a bump, bump, bump, we were down to earth. The plane came to a standstill and I wriggled out. I couldn't believe that a few minutes ago I had been up looking down on the tallest people. I wouldn't have minded going up again.

I was brought back to earth by a big spot of rain. So on went my mac and I climbed onto the seat of the bicycle. My Granddad climbed in beside me and we pedalled up the road.

143   *Anna.* We were to sail July 31st 1961 on the 'Saxonia'. We were to take the train to Montreal. We did so. We mounted the boat and looked at the surroundings. The water lined with oil from the many passing boats. People were bustling about with suitcases and little kids. Many of them were taking their first vacation abroad. Slowly the tug pulled the boat out of the dock. The sights looked quite familiar, I remember thinking of the little change in five years. My brother was full of excitement and exploring everywhere, whereas before, he wasn't old enough to understand. Myself, I felt quite miserable and the idea of leaving, probably never coming back made me even more miserable.

144   *Geraldine.* Then one day, quite a time later we docked in Suez and Jo and I were playing around until we got a bit thirsty. We went on deck to see if mum and dad were having a drink, but they weren't so we went down to our cabins; they weren't there. We searched the ship for what seemed ages, Jo tagging on behind, crying her eyes out and me thinking they had fallen overboard when suddenly we ended up at the nursery and the nurse, seeing Jo crying, took us in.

After a while Jo stopped crying, so I thought I would go out and have another look; but just as we were going out the nurse stopped us and told me to leave Jo in the nursery with her. Jo didn't want to be left alone and I thought if mum, dad and John were drowned I would never leave her, so I had no other choice but to stay. Grown-ups, they'll never understand us.

Lunch-time came and still mum hadn't come to see where we were and the nurse said we could go out as it was lunch-time; so we went on deck to find the others sitting down drinking cokes and beer. We ran up to them and then mum had the cheek to say, 'You look upset about something, dear, do you want a drink?' She ordered two drinks and asked us where we had been. We told her all about it and asked her where they had been. 'Oh, we went on shore', she said very calmly, 'here I've bought two toys for you.'

145 *Leila*. One afternoon Aunt Glad came round to have a parley with mum. I was making a dress for my doll out of an old pair of pyjamas, so when mum said,' Can I tell her?' I naturally looked up, being the only 'her' in the room.

'How would you like to be a bridesmaid for Barbara?' mum said with a smile. 'Will I have a long flowing dress?' I questioned, dancing around the room, swishing my skirt as if wearing a long silken gown.

146 *Angela*. When I saw my sister for the first time after her marriage, I could have jumped for joy. Everything was like olden times, I really was happy. Molly and I was looking and smiling at each other most of the evening, yet we didn't know what to say to each other, till I asked her how she was getting on at her caravan at Stonebridge. When she left I went to bed and had a good cry, not because I was sad, but because I was happy, very happy.

147   *Laura*. When I was about nine or ten my family and I went to visit my nan in London. We went by car and it took us an hour and a half. When we got there I was glad to get out and stretch my legs.

When we got inside and had a big welcome which nans give, I changed into my jeans. Nan gave me one look and said, 'My baby in jeans!' and came over to me and started kissing and pampering me. When I finally got away I went around next door to see a friend who I had known for ages, she was about the same age as me. We decided to go over to the bomb-site where all the kids go to play. As we was walking down the road my mum called out 'be careful'. 'All right,' I answered back. When we got there there was thousands of kids there all like little flies climbing over treacle. They all called out,' Hello Laura,' for I knew nearly all of them.

About half an hour later someone called out,' Look that wall's going to fall any minute!' Everyone stopped what they were doing and looked. A wall that had been left standing was swaying dangerously. 'Run for cover,' they all shouted and belted off down the road.

As my friend and I ran, we tripped over some rubble. Just as we did the wall fell and covered us. All I can remember was a pain and then I went unconscious. Next thing I knew was I was lying in hospital with my head and arms bandaged up and a pain in my side every time I breathed. The first thing I said was 'Margy', for that was my friend's name.

'She's in the next bed,' said the nurse. When I looked she had two broken arms and legs and her head was bandaged up as well. When I looked back again, my parents were there and they tried to comfort me, but they couldn't.

About a week later I was well enough to go home, but Margy had to stay in hospital for two months, because she was partly crippled in one leg where a piece of bone had come right out.

      We stopped in my nan's for another week until I was all right to travel and then went home. The next time I went up there, that was last year, Margy was still limping about, but the bomb-site was now gone and in its place was flats.

148   *Helene.* The last day of the junior school came, the last assembly and the last lessons. At break-time, Iris, Janice and I went round to all the teachers, to say goodbye and to get their autographs.

      It would be the last time we served the teachers their dinners and serving the children through the serving-hatch in the kitchen, where at first we had to have chairs to stand on, so we could see what we were doing. Mr Jackson, who was our teacher, was also leaving, but he was not going to Ashley, which we were all rather glad of, because you can have too much of a good thing — that is when he was in a good temper. He had been quite nice really and he had come to a Guide display especially to see us and brought his wife along too. We had quite a shock for we did not believe he really would go.

      I was not sure if I wanted to leave or not, it would be going from the top of the primary school where you were allowed to look after the tiny ones in the absence of a teacher to the bottom of a secondary modern where you would be treated as if you hadn't any responsibility at all. Only it was not quite like that at all.

149   *Jennifer.* This year one Thursday afternoon we were going to games at Roynton. This day was very cold and windy, so nearly everybody said when they were getting undressed, 'Let's go on strike. It's too cold to play.' At the time nearly everybody agreed to this, but when we arrived at the field only fifteen stuck

it out. I was one of these people and wanted to be called brave and not windy. Mrs Allsop the games teacher told us to run round the field, we all stood there and said nothing.

She then told us to stand against the fence. We all did so. She said, 'I will give you one more chance to run round the field.' Still nobody took any notice. So she said to all of us 'when you get back to school you will all have to see Miss Stokes.' We all said' that will be a very good idea.' So when we arrived back at school, we all had to stand in the hall to wait for Miss Stokes to come. She came downstairs and said to all of us, 'you look very cold indeed.'

So we all had to run round the playground about ten or twelve times. Then we got dressed and went to our next lesson. Before that Miss Stokes said she will see us all tomorrow morning. When tomorrow did come she came to get all the girls that were in this. We had to go in the hall and get a table out and she gave us a pen and paper and we had to write down why we went on strike yesterday. Then again we had to run round the playground. In the afternoon some of the girls were called to see her. My name was one of those to be called to see Miss Stokes. I think in one way she was on our side. Still it was quite funny to go on strike. Now we do not go on strike because most of us have got track suits which are blue and white.

150   *Geraldine.* I was at boarding school and after lights out you're not allowed to talk if you were caught you'd get the slipper.

One night we were telling ghost stories to a weak girl and with torches shone in different colours, water pistols sprayed at her, and there was a terrific din going on. Matron had been in twice already, but this time she came in telling us to put on our slippers and dressing gowns. We were all wondering what was going to happen, when Matron said, 'All right, march over to the Head's house.'

We had to pass the boys' dormitories to get to the house and slowly all the boys' blinds were up and faces peering through them. The headmaster and mistress were told why we were there and the headmistress who had something against us girls said 'cane them.' The Headmaster who liked us better than the boys said, 'no, give them the slipper.'

But as usual Mrs Stevens won and told us to line up, Mr Stevens walked out of the room as the first girl bent over. She got it nine times and came back bawling her eyes out, then Mrs Stevens said, 'Give it to them more and harder.'

I was trembling when it came to my turn, but I walked up to where matron was standing, bent over, gripped my teeth, shut my eyes and — wham, the first one. I thought if I counted maybe I wouldn't feel it so much. I got sixteen and one or two others got eighteen.

We walked back to the dormitories, some crying, some swearing and some trying not to cry. I was trying not to cry, but as soon as I got into bed I burst into tears. Matron came in with glasses of lemonade and handed them round, saying how sorry she was and that she didn't want to cane us but she couldn't argue with the headmistress.

We all had stripes on our backsides the next day and all the boys kept teasing us. We wanted to write about it to our parents, but were forbidden to.

151   *Roger*. It was soon after I started at the Secondary school at Ashley that strange happenings began to alter my life, most remarkable things that I can't explain and I am sure nobody else can. These were happenings that even H. G. Wells could not put pen to paper to explain, these were things concerning heaven

and miracles, spirits and the sub-conscious. I will say no more on this subject. A person must have some secrets.

152   *Paul.* Grandpa was taken ill, the doctor was called in and he said grandpa would have to go into hospital. A few days later I went with mum to a hospital quite near, it had a tall chimney with a black hat on top.

We went in and found grandpa in a little private ward with two beds and a curtain that could be pulled round each bed. As I looked at grandpa there seemed to be something different about him; then I realised what it was, he was all yellow! I was quite shaken up and very scared. I wondered if grandpa knew or if I should tell him. I whispered just in case to mum and she said he had yellow jaundice. Then we sat beside him and talked for about half an hour. I sat a little away from him, in case I should go yellow.

After an operation grandpa went home and we visited him again at his bungalow in Roynton. We visited him almost every week, but I noticed how terribly thin he was getting. Then as Christmas neared he got very ill again and stayed in bed all the time.

That Christmas was the loneliest I had ever spent, or have since. Dad spent all day in Roynton with grandpa. Mum tried to keep me happy, but for those last few weeks I had been well prepared for the worst. That Christmas night was exactly the same as when I was born, bleak and cold with gale force winds sweeping snow before it, packing it up in drifts against the walls of the house.

To make it worse, there was an electric 'cut' and I still have vivid memories of the dark room lit only by flickering coal fire and the equally flickering hurricane lantern. It was very late when I went to bed, but dad had not returned.

In the morning mum came in and told me grandpa had died during the night. I felt a horrible ache in my throat. I tried to swallow but the ache kept on, tears were welling up in my eyes, I bit my lip and swallowed again hard. I did not cry.

I get that same feeling every time I look back on that strange night because grandpa died at 11.40 Christmas night which was when I was born, six years before; he died in the same room on the same kind of night. It was all very strange.

153   *Molly.* I didn't know that my friend had a boy-friend, until one day I couldn't come down as I was going out. She said, 'All right I will see you tomorrow.'

Then I found out that we weren't going out, so I started to walk up to her house. Then I saw it, her and this boy, kissing in the tree. I looked down and started to walk home. She saw me and shouted out, 'Hello, Molly.'

I took no notice and walked on.   She said to the boy, 'She must have seen us.' Next day I didn't talk to her or play. I decided to go and take up dancing lessons like the others.

154   *Jacqueline.* There was a big dance, my mother and father took us along with them. Well, my sister knew how to dance, so this little boy asked her to dance, and that left me sitting all alone, until a boy with black hair and the same height as me said, 'Would you like to dance?' I said, 'I don't dance very well.' He said, 'Don't worry, I will show you how.'

I was getting worried, should I or shouldn't I? I said to myself that it was the last night, why shouldn't I? So I said, 'Yes, I will.'

He took me by the hand onto the dance floor, then he put his arm around me, then we danced. After a time we were both getting bored, so he said, 'Shall we step outside?' I said, ' I don't mind if I do.'

Well, after we walked round and round, he said, 'have you ever been kissed?'

I said, 'N-no.'

He said, 'Would you like me to?'

I thought, well.... Before I could say anything he kissed me. When he had finished, I said, 'Thank you for a nice evening,' and ran off.

The next morning we left and in a way I was glad.

155   *Roger.* As time went on, I gradually started to move away from my parents, I wanted to become independent, but I knew I still depended on them. I began to analyse everything they said to me — began to turn it over and over in my mind until it sounded ridiculous. I also began to get the feeling that only what I said was right and nine times out of ten it wasn't I knew that for a fact.

156   *Jennifer.* I am fourteen years of age and have a boy friend in my form. I will not say what his name is. He sits right near me. We do not talk very much to each other at school because I am very shy of talking to him at school. I have been going out with him for a long time now and I think the world of him. We go to the pictures together sometimes.

Sometimes we go out on our bikes for a ride somewhere nice. I do not go for good-looking boys because looks don't worry me. I go for kindness.

Every morning I get up at six o'clock to do a paper-round. I do not mind getting up early because my mother and father always get up early. I get 13/6d a week paper-round money and 2/6 from my dad. I do fifty four papers a morning. With my money I have bought a record player. Also of course I buy the latest records.

157   *Mary.* I don't know when I first became fond of 'pop' music and singers, but I liked Adam Faith very much. I think I really took up the hobby of collecting pop records and pictures of Adam Faith, Cliff Richard and so on as a sort of defence. David was incessantly talking about football. Whatever subject was being discussed it would sooner or later turn to football!

158   *Angela.* It's funny how you always think it's a shame you couldn't be older, so that you can do more, yet when you're a baby you're too young to do anything and you don't know anything. And when you're older you have to go to school and then you never have enough time to do anything, even when you get a holiday you have to work all the time for your parents. When you leave school you have to go to work, only to have a day off now and then. At nights if you have a boy-friend half the time you didn't know where to go. And a lot of the time you are not alone.

159   *Jennifer.* I am very sure that I will do ladies' hair-dressing. You do not get a lot of money at first. But I don't think money is the only thing in life. I don't think I will get married till I am about nineteen or twenty. So I think I will get somewhere in my career before I get married.

160   *Roger.* Now that I am fourteen years old, I think I have got a fairly good impression of myself. I know what I like and what I don't like. I realise my politics now, I know my opinions. However, what good are my opinions in a world that has not a hundred years to live, because it has already gone too far on the path to self-destruction.

However, whatever happens, I must just keep going, I suppose, but I hope that I never have this period of my life again, I would never stand it!

161   *Marilyn.* Maybe I could continue this book by finding bits of my life that I had missed or that had recently happened—my mind, such as it is, cannot remember anything else. So growing older would be the only way out. This, I will do only in time and by then I would have forgotten about this book long ago.

THE PRINCIPAL CONTRIBUTORS
(Numbers refer to the extracts)

Angela, 92, 98, 112, 138, 146, 158
Annette, 87, 108
Barbara, 44, 50, 61, 68
Brian, 7, 62, 75
Chris, 71, 74, 93
Christina, 113, 115, 133
Christopher, 120, 129
David, 135, 139
Doreen, 21, 23, 29, 46, 107
Eunice, 4, 40, 85, 106
Geraldine, 5, 30, 144, 150
Helene, 36, 63, 91, 148
Jack, 55, 82
Jacqueline, 111, 154
Janet, 1, 22, 31
Janice, 27, 101
Jean, 42, 48, 69, 134
Jennifer, 149, 156, 159
Jim, 39, 131
John, 53, 78, 100, 103
Johnny, 57, 117, 128
June, 70, 140

Ken, 67, 132
Kevin, 14, 64
Laura, 84, 114, 147
Linda, 3, 142
Lucy, 34, 110
Lynne, 11, 32, 41, 94
Malcolm, 43, 45
Marilyn, 6, 105, 161
Mary, 122, 157
Maureen, 12, 18, 56, 60, 73
Molly, 66, 86, 153
Nicholas, 10, 19, 33, 90
Paul, 20, 24, 141, 152
Pauline, 2, 54
Raymond, 15, 51, 80, 83, 97
Richard, 13, 65
Roger, 77, 96, 109, 136, 151, 155, 160, Section 2
Roy, Section 2
Sally, 119, 137
Sue, 47, 89
Suky, 79, 121
Valerie, 26, 28, 76

NOTE ON SECTION ONE

By the end of their second year at the school, the children had written accounts (largely as a result of the 'Listening and Writing' Schools Broadcasts) of moving house, starting primary school, and other experiences. At this point I said something like: 'Next year, for the main work of one term, you are going to write me the story of your life, filling a complete exercise book' (gasps from some). 'This doesn't mean that you'll do more written work. In place of each composition you'll do one chapter — you'll see, you'll manage it.'

They did. One girl wrote a hundred and forty sides and could plainly have gone on indefinitely. Another, whose usual preoccupations included ripping soap dispensers out of the wall, wrote twenty-two civilised sides one wet Sunday. Even the gang leader (mentioned in Section 2), 'W.P.', wrote well about a childhood full of illness which had had one high spot: a newspaper photograph with Princess Margaret when she visited his hospital.

The sheer length of the work was beyond only the remedial 10 per cent, and some of those children managed the longest piece of writing of their careers — as much as fifteen sides before they tired. The rest managed at least half a book and most did much more.

One boy took advantage of the escape clause which I allowed them and wrote (very badly) about someone else. One parent objected, out of the four hundred over the two years. The others welcomed the work. In some cases, I think, it actually made things go more smoothly at home — children heard what beautiful babies they were and listened sympathetically to their parents' reminiscences.

I gave out new writing books and began to tell them about when I was a boy; where I used to live; my earliest recollection; things I did not remember, but had been told about. About ten minutes of that — then they wrote and wrote.

The writing was going along steadily, but its reading had to be organised. With the small remedial class, reading, writing and talking about the work went on at the same time. For the other classes, the arrangement was a much more formal one. I asked them to produce a minimum of ten sides a fortnight, allowing the A stream one lesson a fortnight to write in class, the B's one lesson a week; the rest was done at home. I staggered the supply so that it came in weekly and the work was, in theory, complete by either the twelfth or the thirteenth week. I gave no direct help during the writing.

I looked forward to my three hundred pages of manuscript a week. That is the only secret, such as it is: I found what the children had written completely absorbing, almost every word of it. Of course, knowing the children gave an extra dimension to the reading — but rather in the way that one would be doubly interested in a friend's novel, not out of nosiness rewarded. What the children chose to remember and record was as interesting as the actual details of their stories.

The level of attainment was surprisingly even. Children who were not normally ' good' at English found that the right words came when there was something to say; those who did not normally write at length found fluency once they were warmed up. Stories were told in a leisurely characterful way — assured, but unostentatious. One felt the writers were growing up and that this sustained piece of thought and writing had helped them to do so.

I would spend a lesson or more giving back each section of the work, saying something to the class about what each boy or girl had written — reading the best bits, as much as a chapter at a time; summarising what I had no time to read; encouraging them to read each other's stories. After forty-odd minutes one-way talk I would feel pretty tired: not good teaching method, yet the children were agog for more and came to look on this session as their due for work well done.

Their autobiographies were more than long compositions, though; they were collages, compilations, works of art. They contained photographs, reports, work from the infant school, drawings — and in one case a baptismal certificate. From the beginning I had made it clear that the books were the property of the writers — I would keep them at the end if they would otherwise be thrown away. I stipulated merely that when the book was complete the parts I liked best should be copied out so that I could make some sort of collection.

I do not know what was the size of the total *œuvre* — at a conservative estimate, some 600,000 words. This, when the extracts had been copied, was reduced to about a thousand 'best' pages. From that selection I picked out the samples of writing by nearly seventy children out of the original two hundred — A, B and C streams are represented, though I admit that something over half the extracts are from the 'top-end' of the year.

*

2008: *Had there been photocopiers in UK schools in the early Sixties, I suppose I would have used them to preserve examples of children's writing. However, that would not necessarily have meant that they had positive feelings about such a process — or even were aware of it. In the case of* Fourteen *the principle of preserving 'best work' in handwritten form was not only agreed, but regarded as a privilege. An age of innocence, I suppose.*

SECTION TWO

Roy who had 'problems' was friendly and hard-working, though sometimes in his eye there was a mad flicker. At school the thing he liked to do most was tidy the English stock cupboard. Happy to remain at the foot of the B form, he did well to produce his eighteen frank and jumbled sides.

Roger, careful, reasonable, interested, was 'good at English'. I have used seven extracts from his autobiography in the previous section. Yet his 'life' was far from being the most entertaining — it was, simply, different. There is a reflective quality about the work, something un-spontaneous — style is often in control of what is said.

I think that a fourteen-year-old more academic than Roger might be too much on guard, too literary, to write a lively and individual life story. On the other hand, a boy or girl less literate than Roy would not have the necessary stamina, would be too unsatisfied at what was produced.

The autobiographies of Roger and Roy were ' the outer limits' of the exercise — they are, respectively, the most literary and the most incoherent of those which were successfully completed. Both life stories are given in full below, exactly as written — except for place-names and surnames, which have been altered or suppressed.

Roy: MY AUTOBYOGRAPHY.

      This story start from as far as I can remember.
      It is set out in paragraph's.

When I was born I was very dark in eyes a slightly in my skin.
I was born in ashley in my mum's own bed from that day on I cant remember any thing till the day I was chrisened at Donnington church, at the age of 5 I remember having a tug-o-war which happed to envolve a mouse which was dead and a stupid brother, we held the mouse aftter getting it out of the trap and had a fight over it and it ended in a tug of war and I ended up holding the skin of it's tail my brother had got the body of it but another fight started and we decided to share it and so in the end we cut up the dead mouse and buried in two different place's to tell the truth I did not mind cutting up the mouse.

Chapter 2.

A week later the Chickens got aroused as it was Sunday we all ran to the end of the garden to find a large rat biting at the Chickens we all got a large stick to try and kill it but I was different I got my gun that shot plastic ball's and when the rat ran out I was pumping out all the balls scaring the rat out of its skin but none of the Six people got it when I was seven year's old I started too help my father everd day I come home from school all I used to do was to get nails out of old soles or get down some new soles and heels or even get costomer's shoes my father told me the coluor, ladies or men, and the name and style, every morning I polished my shoes on my dad machine

Shoe Cleaner

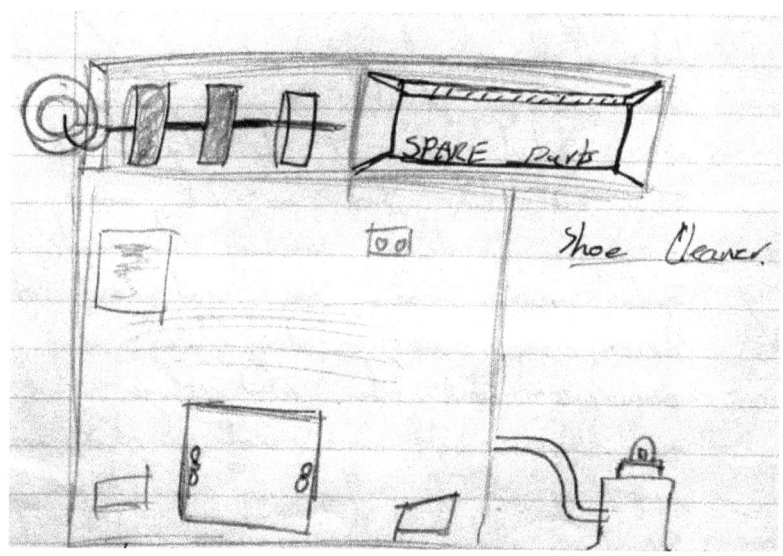

Although, it was rather fun helping my father and when I had finshed I helped my mum with her shopping, one morning on the way to school I found a large tortoise going for a walk up bellwood road I picked it up and whent home with it I called it nobby also I had some gunia-pig's who later had babies all wrapped up in skin most of them were black and brown with white feet not long after the white gunia-pig got killed it was our own fault it could not be helped also at the top of the garden in our shed lived our white mouse who very soon produced something like eighteen smaller ones these soon got out of the box and got flying about everywhere about the rather large shed we Never caught one and everytime we went up to the Shed we was bound to see a white baby mouse climbing about here or there but now I set off for School finding out that I was just in time the lesson's there were not to bad the school I think was

built about 1803 this piece of numbering was to be seen right on the front of the school At home time I went out a got my trolly which was hidden in an old building it was all down hill on the way back and once or twice I could roll at quite a speed into my back garden and crash into the old wooden fence which later was changed to another type of fencing before tea we went through a hole into the Congregational church at the end of the garden we climbed a tree and onto the Church roof whic was flat on two side's and ordanairy house shaped in the middle we used this to be our head quaters and used to bombard passing enemies Sometimes we got a lucky shot and hit them on the back of the head there was two proper ways down one by diving at a tree that we come up or down the old drainpipe in the corner but if we decided to tRy and Jump we was quite welcome later on Saturday we would go down to jones and blenkin-sopps to by a box of stink bomb's the we would run over to the pub and throw two in this caused quite a disturbance but we never minded round the corner of the pub was many windowledes on these we found beer glasses and we took them into the pub and got a bag of crisps for bringing in the glasses, after throwing the rest of the stink bombs int the police station and running I went to the pub yard for a game of foot-ball with Johny Stenson.
Sometimes we played tennis on the roof this was rather fun. On Sunday we went down to the beach at walton-on-the-naze this is where there are many cliffs. Talking off cliffs I went for a climb on one that had a curve in the middle when I got to the top I lost my grip and fell the cliff was just over the height of a house, when I Came to a decent landing spot I pretended that I was flying but It must have been a flying saucer for I landed on Someones tea Cup which crunched up under my weight, after this I went on the small boats which was very exciting, they looked like this

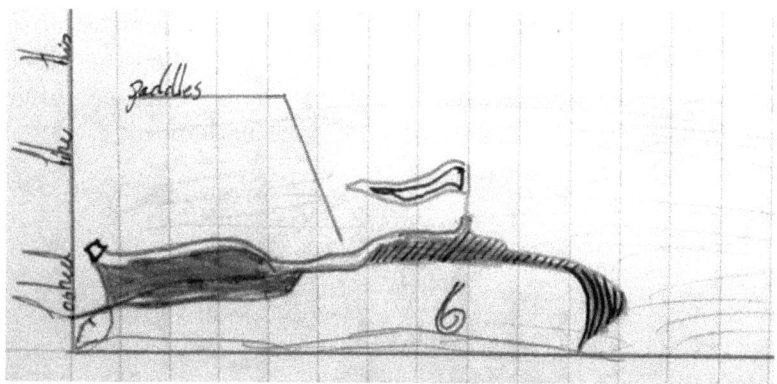

Thursday 10th This was quite fun until you had to go in after all this I cant remember much so what I know I will tell you, when my father was playing golf me and my fat headed brother were sitting down when Suddenly the deckchair went and I was laying on the grownd whith a Crushed hand and bawling my head of That ruined the day because we all went down to the Island for a small stay at the beach when we was there I went swimming (Like a brick) anyway there was a lot of Jelly fish down there and I found won washed up on the shore and I stuck my finger right through it. I did'ent mind doing that and So I prodded it Quite a lot and when it come for a meal it thought about what I had been doing and was put off almost immediately by the thought it was beginning to get very hot and so I went, and dug a hole in the ground (by the Sea) and Jumped in then I made a hole or ditCh from the Sea and the hole got filled with water and I kept Cool and almost dozed off when a man jumped into the hole and I got a good ducking until the man got off me and apologized and also bought me an Ice cream and then I ran back to find my parents who were looking for crabs under the rocks finding none until suddenly something wich looked like a stone crawled across the sea bed I Ran and caught it but it bit me and so I chucked a stone on it and killed it all in spite of it biting me the following day I fell and broke my wrist and had to go to hospital after several visits I Came to the day when the plaster was taken off and they used = sciscors Clippas and a new thing that looked like this drawing which follows underneath

As Today is November the 5th I will talk about our firer-work fun. That night it was raining and we was beggiining to get upset yes upset only because our mum and dad would not Come out until our brother derek got home we all went outside and watched other people's firework's going off i.e. Catherine weel's AiR bom's AeRoplane golden Rain golden fleece and Rockets flying and make couloured balls and bangs sparklers were being held by the youngsters bangers flying here there and evrywhere, Jack-in-the box's flue evrywhere mount Everest whith it white-blue-and red flame meltet To its base Roman Candals shot balls that lit up and then went out Some fireworks Shot small whistles into the aiR I called them screamers I was thinking how lucky those people where when a large rocket CRacked in the air i Ran inside and got a Rocket out of my own box and let it off It wasent much fun being by yourself wathing Someone els'es fireworks Suddenly a van pulled up outside and I Ran though the back gate but it wase'nt my brother Come home from work

  My head was aching In my stomach and my eyes must have been gleaming Just waiting waiting and waiting waiting waiting getting sick Just sick enough in the head to be devilish I wanted to do Something bad but I Couldent So I yelled out loud Some word umensiable and I Ran at a wall and Clamberd up it like a cat I was in a temper my cat passed by and I was going to Jump on it and squeze his eyballs out but my brother come though the gate I jumped and jumped From wall to dustbin to ground and Tried to run in the gate but Someone bolted it I got on the dust bin and flew like tarzan on a vine and shot half way over the gate and unbolted it for my brother who walked in and left me Clambering down the gate until I Reached the botton of the gate I Ran inside yelling for my parents to Come outside They all walked outside everbody except Dad was Running to the garden but before the got there, I put a Jumping CRacker on the gravel path and it CRacked all over the paths this Started the firework night of Nov 5th 1962 and now I am waiting for Christmas. When I started school my first problem was w.p. and his stupid gang the Second Was malcolm —.
The School dinner's here are no where neaR as good as my favorite dinner at hornchurch The dinners at ashley which were my favourites still did not Compare whith the dinners at my old school which were one hard boild eggs cold and chips whilh School if you got in on the last Table you would propably get Seconds the dinners at the other school Costed the same price as they do here, there was was also a lot of fun down at the aiRpoRt my Class at that School was 2B)

Roger: THE STORY OF AN ORDINARY.

CH. 1.

I was born fourteen years ago in Ashley. I think I will ignore the months, as much as possible, I feel they make a story such as this sound too formal.

It never really occurred to me what I was, and where I was living until I was about four or five years old. My life seemed to start as a hazy blur, which, as the years progressed, gradually came into focus. At that age the image became sharp, I realised where I was and who I was. I was at peace with the world at this age. This was the age of eternal sunshine and summer. All my recollections of this early age are happy ones.

When on my own, though small, I felt I knew everything. I was ten feet tall and felt every inch of it. Until confronted with someone over four feet high, a grown up. When this occurred I started to feel shy, and when people spoke to me, I could feel my face getting redder and redder. I never answered people if they spoke to me, in fact my mother usually ended up apologising to the person for me being so dumb and shy. Whenever she did this I felt like showing the world that I wasn't shy, nor afraid of people. I never did though. And so I just remained a patronised little boy, perhaps that is why I do so hate patronising people now. A person like this came into my life later, though I did not know it then.

This little escapade took place when I was about five years old, or I may have been slightly older. I was thoroughly fed up at the time, and had nothing to do. Suddenly I remembered what our next door neighbour had said the previous day. She told my mother that if she wanted to she could come over and collect some windfalls from her apple trees. So I decided to make use of this, I thought I would pretend to be one of those famous commandos that you see in the comics and on television. As well as being good fun I thought, I would be helping my mother out by collecting apples for her.

So thinking my neighbour would not mind, I crept on my hands and knees through the fence, and into her garden, which, by the way, was very large.

I was on a dangerous mission, the enemy was only a few yards away, or so it seemed to me. I was now trapped in a large minefield, I could not turn back. Well I could really, but I didn't want to because that would spoil the game.

I picked up a few apples, from right under the nose of the enemy. But suddenly the enemy, our neighbour emerjed from her headquarters. Was it the end! Agent 15X5 that was my under cover name, was faced with a terrible doom. My capture meant disaster to England. I started to clamber to my feet, waiting for the moment of agony. However instead of gunning me down, the enemy started to walk towards me.

Then the bubble in which I had been shrouded since the beginning off my game, popped. I was back in the world of reality. In the seconds that followed I began to realise what was happening. Our next door neighbour had seen me. I thought she was going to give me a good telling off. However, instead she patted me on the head in a very patronising way, glared at me, and helped me pick up some more apples. But it wasn't the same as doing it myself, as an under-cover agent.

Nearly in tears I walked back to my house, across the minefield, knowing full well that my secret mission had been a failure.

CH. 2.

I was now at such an age as to be ready to start school. My school life started at a small, infants school in Creswell.

My mother escorted me on the first day, and the first day only, I didn't want my classmates thinking that I wasn't able to come to school without my mother's assistance.

The morning of my first day at school was a very cold one. In fact it was snowing.

There were only two classes in the school, and which class you were put in was determined by your age not by your intelligence. As I have already said, this school was very small, but it did not seem so to me. As it was my first school I suppose this was only to be expected.

During my early school life, the age of eternal sunshine that I spoke of earlier, began to be broken by a few stormy-looking clouds that were appearing on the horizon.

Most of my free time during school time was taken up with playing cowboys and Indians, a game that will never die, for it has no boundaries. Our battlefield was a flat expanse of grass about 50 yards wide and the same long. I will never forget those marvelous charges we used to have, in the best traditions of the old west. Some of them, however, did get a little rowdy, sometimes, these charges became more like a massacre and ferocious six-year olds became locked in a pitched and bloody battle, in which only the biggest survived. Surprisingly few were hurt.

During my stay at this school, I entered an Art Competition. I knew that I had never won anything before, and was not likely to now, anyway I had a go.

About six weeks later, I was sent for. For a moment I thought I was going to be told off for something, before being told otherwise—I walked into the other class room, the larger of the two. The children in the room had obviously been told to clap as I walked in, for they would never, never, do it of there own accord. When they started to clap, I could feel myself blushing terribly, a hot shiver went through me. I was led up to the desk at the far end of the class room. There a tall lady was standing. I was told to shake hands with her. I did so and she promptly placed in my hand a back of sweets and a sixpence. A consolation prize for the competition that I had entered, six weeks before.

I was rather disappointed because of the result of my painstaking efforts, and this affair was quickly forgotten and soon disappeared into the mists of time.

Before my stay at this school ended, there occured one incident that I can remember most vivedly. It was all over one game of marbles.

It was a wet afternoon. The rain had stopped just a few minutes before our afternoon break. There was to be a great game of cowboys and Indians, that afternoon, but because of the recent rain, we were forbidden to use the field. So we had to resort to marbles, tame though it was.

I was not feeling in a very sociable mood that afternoon, and all through that game of marbles I kept having arguments with my opponent. One argument to many eventually occured. It was a dispute over who should have a marble, that I claimed he had won by foul means. There followed the most frightful row, which led to us taking the marble and the argument to our form teacher. A wise old bird if ever there was one.

She listened to both our stories. Each one being equally convincing to her mind. Eventually she came to a conclusion, she said she would cut it in half. We both protested to this rash move. If it was cut in half it wouldn't be any good to either of us.

I'm sure that all the time she knew she could not cut the marble in half, but we did not. Eventually the problem was finally solved. The marble was confiscated, and so ended this little incident.

A few weeks after the marble affair, it came to my notice that I had served my time at this school, and that I was to leave in a few days. A tingling sense of alarm spread from my feet upwards. The boys at the bigger school up the hill might be bullies. If they were, what was to become of little old me!!

CH. 3.

My first day at the bigger school up the hill, turned out to be a case of history repeating itself. It was snowing. The nature of the day was not unlike the feeling that was in my mind at the time—a feeling of intense gloom and depression.

By the next, however, I had cheered up considerably, so had the weather. It turned out to be quite pleasant.

On this particular day, it so happened that a wooden hut was just being erected. By this hut was a pile of hot, sticky tar. On the tar was stuck a white handkerchief. I can remember standing for hours, well for quite a long time anyway, watching this handkerchief being enveloped by the tar. I watched it until it completely disappeared from my gaze. Believe it or not, during my whole stay at this school, this is the one incident I can remember most vivedly.

The favourite winter pass time at this school, was undoubtly racing minature cars—racing cars of course. This was a noble art indeed. The smooth tarmac of the driveway provided a perfect place for the practise of this fascinating pastime. All went well until somebody decided to walk up the drive. When this occured, the victim would find himself ankle deep in racing cars, much to the disgust of the people who sent them on their way. This treatment was not exactly the ideal thing for a corn sufferer.

Two months later, during one of our take it easy, do nothing, lessons, it was decided by our rather weak-willed teacher, that we were to make these sort of flat faces on sticks. Peculiar things. They were made out of plain cardboard, the features being crayoned on after the head was stuck to the handle.

As it happened, in the end, my face did not turn out very well. The person sitting next to me, however, did quite a good one. I suppose I must admit it—I was jealous. He showed the teacher his face-on-a-stick and was highly praised for it. The boy began to walk back to his seat, his face beaming. It was then that I had a most evil idea. As he was sitting down, I noticed that he had applied his wax crayon to the face, very heavily.

My friend was a very gullible person. Taking advantage of this, I then proceeded to convince him that he would obtain a much better effect than he had, by scraping off the surplus wax with his finger nails. He thought it was a marvelous idea and he immediately put the plan into practise.

When he had got half way down the head, he exclaimed that it was not turning out as I said it would. I reassured him by telling him that it looked far better when all of it had been scraped. So he continued scraping intently. At last he finished and let out a cry of dismay. Howling obsenities at me, he went out to show the teacher. She sympathised with him, but the damage had been done. I sympathised with him also, I took pity on his gullible character and was from then on thankful that I was not like he.

CH. 4.

Although I have said a lot about my school life, I feel you must bear in mind that a lot of the more important incidents of my life took place out of school time.

The first happening that is worth writing about occurred when I was about eight years old, or something like that anyway. We were living at our old house in Ashley at the time.

Next door to us a bungalow was being erected. All round this bungalow was a pathway of boards supported about 6 ft. off the ground by scaffold poles.

After the workmen had gone home, my brother and I often used to run round the site on these boards. One day however, there was a gap left in the boards by the workmen. Whilst chasing each other around I forgot about the gap. I went charging forward, disappeared through the hole and landed about 6 inches away from some steel pipes. I couldn't remember much else except a man rushing across the road to help me. Somehow I had cut my head. I never went near that building site again. It had scarred my memory for life.

When it was decided that this bungalow was to be built, a huge willow tree that used to stand there had to be pulled down. This willow tree was so huge that when it was at its leafiest, it used to blot out the sunlight and this made our living room very dark in summer. In Autumn, however we regained some of the light that during the summer months, would have filtered out of existence by the Willow's leaves.

During the winter months our garden used to be covered in willow leaves, some green some yellow, and some of the older ones, brown. I remember taking these leaves and floating on our water butt by the side of our house. I pretended these leaves were boats and I used to kick the sides of the butt so as to create little waves which shook the leaves on the water.

The old willow tree holds other memories for me as well, though. During the years it was standing, my brother and I climbed it many times. We used to have such adventures in it.

On one very windy day, my brother and I decided to climb the willow tree. Believe me it was windy. We climbed the tree, and clambered about amongst its branches. They were creaking tremendously. The wind through the leaves was deafening, it was like crawling across one of the spars on the mast of a clipper while a 70 m.p.h. gale was blowing. Most exhilarating! Although I have never practised this feat I could guess what it was like.

During the next few months quite a lot happened in the way of new games being invented. The first originated at school. It consisted mainly of warfare—of course. There were few in our gallant band, in fact the only one I can remember who was on our side was Malcolm —.

We were always greatly outnumbered in these battles, but that made it even more fun.

The second game was akin to the first but was formed out of school time. It followed roughly the form of " cops and robbers". The area of the chase—all ashley, mostly the backroads were used. Usually these chases lasted for hours and ended in a punch up.

For as long as I can remember, I have had a sort of Phobia about the sea. This became most evident to me in a holiday we spent about five years ago in Jaywick.

My brother has always liked the sea, unlike me, and whenever he gets the chance he always goes in. I was usually left standing on the beach. Watching. Sometimes I went in, but you could only call it paddling really. I remember pretending to like the sea, I even used to try to convince myself sometimes, but deep down I had a secret loathing of it. As I say I often used to tell my Father that I loved the sea. I probably did this because I was jealous of my brother. However just because I disliked the sea it didn't spoil my holiday one little bit. I could have just as much fun on dry land.

There is a lot about Jaywick I remember, but most vivedly I think, I can remember the sea wall. The shape of the slabs and where it was crumbling. I remember walking along the hot concrete roads. I remember the dust.

All the little holiday chalets near the sea front were situated along a series of avenues at the back of which was a road, a rubbish tip, and a stagnant pond. Now there are two— The old boating pool has falling into disuse since.

I can remember well lying awake in our chalet in Alvin avenue, listening to the sea against the sea wall. First a roll like thunder, then a gentle splashy patter in contrast, as the spray hit the road.

When we were not down on the beach, we often used to play cricket in the avenue. I used to cheat terribly. I used to tell the person bowling to roll the ball along. I consequently scraped the bat along the ground so that I couldn't miss. If it did, and it hit the wicket I used to swear blue murder.

One year, after our stay at Jaywick, we went to stay with my uncle for a while. We also took our dog, a huge golden Labrador weighing 98 lbs. whilst at my uncles, I caught some fish from a big pond on the common. When it was time to leave my uncle's house I put them in an 'OXO' tin. what with the shaking the van and the efforts of our dog to reach the fish, the tin developed a leak, consequently I had to bung it up with a piece of paper. Just as a matter of interest, the fish died soon after we arrived home.

CH. 5.

A majority of this chapter deals with speed in one form or another.

When I was about ten years old, a friend of my Father's called at our house. With him he had a 650 c.c. Triumph 'Thunderbird', motorbike. My brother and I fell in love with it straight away. I suppose the man realised this, for he offered to take us for a ride. My brother went first. When he got back, he told me to get on. Seeing as my brother thought it was wonderful, I thought I had nothing to lose. Except my life. For the man was by no means a safe rider. All I remember of that ride was clinging on to his leather jacket until my hands became soaked with sweat. I was petrified. He drove at a speed eight times the number of years I had lived. Never was I so glad to get home again.

A few weeks later, however, we saw him again. This time with a car, as he had recently smashed up his motor bike. My brother, Father and I, accepted a lift from him, as we were waiting for a bus in Stechford square. He proved to be just as reckless with a car as a motor bike, for he took us home at way above the 70 m.p.h. mark. Speed limit or no speed limit. Though I admit I did urge him on a bit.

The second incident relating to speed, concerned my brother and his cycle. I was as yet not old enough to ride the sort of cycle he had. A Lentern racer with dropped handlebars that were covered in bright red tape. It wasn't a very marvelous bike, I realise that now, but it looked wonderful to me at the time.

My brother often used to come into the house, his face bright red and laced with sweat and foaming at the mouth. He then used to tell us how fast he had ridden. It was often somewhere up in the 4o's, for my brother had the policy that I have since adopted: Flat out or nothing!

Whenever he used to tell us all of his feats, I used to watch the expression on my mother's face, it was an expression of inner pain and torture, for I knew that she hated it to know how fast he had been. All she could do was to wait until the day he would gain one mile an hour too many and crash.

That crash never came. I only hope I am just as lucky, for since those days I have fulfilled my dream of having a racing bike of my own. Indeed my bike is better than my brother's was as far as speed is concerned.

My third and final experience of speed at this age, was in connection with soap-box carts. I was not so lucky with accidents in this field, I have the scars to prove it. But all the same it was good fun while it lasted. The soap-box cart era holds one profound memory for me. The day, whilst careering down a hill, the front wheel hit a rock. The axle was ripped clean away from the floorboards, and the whole cart somersaulted. Surprisingly I wasn't hurt!

CH. 6.

Back to school for my next chapter. I was still only about ten years old, but pushing eleven.

It was about this time the assembly hall was being built. I remember well, looking at the modern-looking triangular-shaped concrete pillars oulined against the sky. In fact I often think that the superstructure was more pleasing to the eye than the finished building.

The remainder of the time I spent at this school was quite a pleasant period. The field was very nice at this school when it was dry, and many enjoyable games of football and cricket were had on it.

The school had few teachers, most of which were quite tame and friendly especially Mr. —; who everybody liked. We often worked on models with him, also lino-cuts and similar handicrafts were practiced by some of us who went into his form room Friday dinner times, we had sandwiches for dinner usually.

Our headmaster wasn't so bad as headmasters go. For instance, the one before Mr. —, was a right terror, literaly. He well an truly put the wind up me I can tell you.

Perhaps one of my most vivid memories of my stay at this school was when, one day I put a tack on the chair of poor old Miss —, she took us for all the subjects that would generally come under the category of 'miscelaneous'. Alas she found me out for this prank in due course, and she didn't even sit on it either.

Poor old Miss — put up with hell when she took class four, us. She sometimes used to take us for a news lesson, usually be the end of the lesson, half her news paper cuttings, that she so neatly laid out on the table, were missing. They we usually to be found, however, in the waste paper basket, torn up.

On the whole, my stay at this school was more enjoyable than at the infant school. Whenever it was fine we were able to take out equipment from the sport's shed, all these sorts of things make a school a more enjoyable place. My next school, however, lacked these things, that is why the next year of my school life proved to be the most unhappy one.

However, before I pass on to the time I spent at Roynton Secondary School, there is an incident I feel I must tell.

I mentioned before the games we had out of school time, most of these games started on a vacant plot of land at the back of Malcolm —'s house. We often used to play football here. One game of football I will never forget.

One boy who we were playing with once, played in full kit, and at the end of the game we worked out a plot to pinch his trousers. We did so and threw in an old pit at the bottom of the field. He ended up pleading with us for the return of his trousers.

CH. 7

I felt sad when I had to leave the school at Ashley, I had heard nasty rumours about the boys and masters at the Roynton school.

Before I started at this school, I was bought my first pair of long trousers—I thought they were wonderful.

My first day was uneventful and boring. I drew my opinions of the school in this first day. I didn't like it. However you were able to buy ice creams at dinner time and sit on the wall and eat them.

Life at the school rapidly fell into a groove an unbroken groove, no outings no nothing. The only thing I did enjoy were the Art lessons. We had a nice art teacher. So nice in fact that he once took Alan — and I to an Art Exhibition in London one Saturday morning, we also visited The' Cutty Sark' at Greenwich. This is about all I have to say about this school.

I was about thirteen when I began to form my own beliefs—both political and to an extent religious, it was also about this age that I began to have fits of supreme happiness. Why I had them I don't know. One minute I was quite normal and the next I felt wonderful and very happy, as I say, why I do not know.

When I was about thirteen and a half my brother bought his first motor bike. I always vowed I would never sit on the back of a motor bike again, but in the end I gave in. I suppose deep down I have a profound liking for motorbikes, mainly due to their speed I suppose. I remember being scared stiff the first time I went out with my brother. Whenever he went fast I used to close my eyes, so that all could feel was the vibration of the bike, and the smell of his leather jacket filled my nostrils.

My brother's motor bike I must say came in very handy as far as getting to school was concerned, the school I was attending at this time was the new school in Ashley—a secondary school, in fact I still attend this school.

Ashley school contrasted greatly with Roynton. At Ashley, it was we who were top dogs, there were no prefects to order you about, there were things to break the monotony of the time table, this school was altogether better.

It was soon after I started at the Secondary school at Ashley that strange happenings began to alter my life, most remarkable things, things that I can't explain and I am sure nobody else can. These were happenings that even H. G. Wells could not put pen to paper to explain, these were things concerning heaven and miracles, spirits and the sub-conscious. I will say no more on this subject. A person must have some secrets. About a year ago a rumour went round that we were to move house.

None of our family really wanted to move, we all had friends here. Also we had no say in the matter.

We moved on the same day that Yuri Gagarin, the Russian Cosmonaut, made his Space flight.

The rumour proved to be true, we were to be moved to Roynton. None of our family really wanted the move, we all had friends here. Alas we had no say in the matter.

We moved on the same day that Yuri Gagarin, the Russian Cosmonaut made his Space flight.

Right from the start, I hated living in Roynton, but I had one thing to be grateful for, I was still able to attend Ashley school, I would have hated to go back to Roynton school.

For the first two months, I traveled to school by train. I soon got fed up with this however, and turned to my cycle as a means of transport. I enjoyed travelling by bike more than by train, except when it rained of course, and I soon began timing myself from Roynton high street to the school. In time, the distance between the school and home, got shorter and shorter. The strange thing is I never seemed to get tired of the journey, nor of the scenery.

As time went on, I gradually started to move away from my parents, I wanted to become independent, but I knew I still depended on them. I began to analyse everything they said to me—began to turn it over and over in my mind until it sounded ridiculous. I also began to get the feeling that only what I said was right and nine times out of ten it wasn't, I knew that for a fact.

As I grew older, I tended to look back into the past rather than the future, I don't why I did this, perhaps it was because I was afraid of what was to come. Most of the things I looked back on were pleasant, some of course, were not, but now they are all left behind, the good and the bad—left behind to gather dust and cobwebs.

Just for a page or so, lets blow away the dust and see just what I can remember:

I can remember going for long walks with my Father, and Peter, our dog. What a wonderful dog he was. I will never forget the day we had to have him destroyed.

On Thursday, the twelfth of February, he became terribly ill with a heart attack. I remember lying on my bed, shaking and crying, I knew what was to follow.

On Friday the thirteenth of February, he had to be destroyed. I left the house for four hours whilst the vet. was there. I had never felt so miserable before. What year all this took place in I don't know. But enough of this, let's find something more pleasant.

For instance, I remember all the fun I used to have with orange boxes. I used to make submarines and aeroplanes, lorries and cars out of them. I remember making pots out of clay, dams out of mud. I remember going to pick cherries with my mother and Father. I also have hundreds of memories of 'Bonfire' nights, happily spent, I remember one year, it didn't light.

I expect I have lots of other memories if I look back far enough, but who wants to? I would rather forget.

Now that I am fourteen years old, I think I have got a fairly good impression of myself. I know what I like and don't like. I realise my politics now, I know my opinions. However, what good are my opinions in a world that has not a hundred years to live because it has already gone too far on the road to self-destruction.

However what ever happens I must just keep going I suppose, but I hope I never have to live this period of my life again, I would never stand it!

NOTE ON SECTION TWO

2008: *Roy's drawings in Section 2 are reproduced for the first time, as is the facsimile paragraph from Roger, in which he neatly tells of a change in his own 'ordinary' life in 1961 – in the context of a cosmic human event.*

Roy was badly behind with the work to begin with: two sides only were produced during the first fortnight, but then he got on well, as his date 'Thursday 10th' (October) and the reference to bonfire night show. As you might guess, Roger's account ends precisely on the last line of the final page of the exercise book.

Roy's ambiguous syntax, time scale, and calligraphy (as in the November 5th entry) are, where not fortuitous, instinctive. On the other hand, Roger's manuscript, though there are few crossings out, shows thought about style — he has taken particular care to avoid repetition of words and phrases.

Differences may be observed between Roger's work in Section 1 and the 'same' passages in their context. The Section 1 examples were transcribed from the boy's copies (which were supposed to be exact) while the complete life-story comes from his original 'book'. Roger, being something of a perfectionist, could not resist minor improvements.

Roger has something of a gift for the pithy saying: 'scarred my memory', 'eight times the number of years I had lived', 'only the biggest survived'. This last example is deliberately reminiscent of Darwin. His sources do show (whereas Roy, needless to say, has not read Salinger and Carlos Williams): the cliché into the mists of time' is remembered from *The Otterbury Incident* (where it is used in imitation of a boy's style!), while the protectively mock-heroic tone of much of the writing comes from his friends John, Ken and Malcolm.

It is interesting that Malcolm should be mentioned in both accounts and fairly easy to see that Malcolm would be Roger's friend and Roy's tormenter. The age gap of a year is important here, of course. Roy was in 3B from 1962 to 1963, Malcolm and Roger in 3A from 1961 to 1962.

References in Roger's account and elsewhere make it necessary to explain that the original third year had begun their education at the large Roynton school and then elected to transfer at the end of their first year. Roy's contemporaries had come direct from primary schools to the Ashley secondary school.

Roy, although an Ashley boy, had lived elsewhere for a time. His previous school had nothing good to say about him, but back in Ashley he reserved his delinquency for out of school hours.

Obviously Roger is one of the most capable members of the secondary modern group. But, while his command of English is rather better than that of some trainee teachers, it is by no means phenomenal. One does occasionally come across 'the phenomenal' — even in the modern school. I will quote one representative sentence written by a first-year boy with a bad stammer: '"Good morning, Miss Logan," said the class, inserting a hyphen between each syllable.'

One final example may serve to show how this business of writing about oneself may be developed. Here is Lynne (see extracts 11, 32, 41, 94) experimenting with style.

2008: *Overleaf is a facsimile of part of her work.*

Inside the church on the right hand side of the is a holy water stoop. There is a rather musty atmosphere; this is due to the lingering smell of incense in all principle church services (such as mass).

The organ started to play and we sung "Ye Holy Angels Bright". The organ which was formally a barrel organ was purchased for £60 in 1900.

Father Morgan went up to the altar, which had two large candles, one on each side of it, crossed himself and began –

"Let us pray. The Lords prayer. Our father which art in heaven –"

"I feel sick" said a little boy behind me. So there was a shuffle of chairs and the little boys mother took him out.

The service went on for an hour with singing and prayers. The choirboys then went out in their shining white surplices, one spreading incense as he went out, followed by Father Morgan blushing more than ever.

CONCLUSION

The choirboys slowly walked down the aisle in their white surplices. The eldest-looking choirboy was throwing incense round the church, highly perfumed. The sun gleamed through the great mosaic windows which had pictures of Our Lady and St. John carved beautifully on them. The vicar walked in front of the small procession with a big cross. He was tall, middle-aged and wore glasses, he was blinking as if he was short-sighted.

Father —, the vicar, said a short prayer and then we sang 'Praise My Soul the King of Heaven'. He then started to preach. I was listening, although it wasn't making much sense, my mind was thinking about something else. About going out and playing with my friends down our street, going for a picnic, riding on my bike, when —

'Almighty and everlasting God, who hatest nothing that Thou hast made'— suddenly made me come to. I realised everyone else was on their knees praying. I blushed a little and got down quickly.

The sun glared through the huge mosaic window putting a flicker of light on the nave.

The church consists of a nave, north aisle, west tower, small porch and vestry. The walls are composed of mixed rubble and ragstone and the roof is tiled. The west tower has an embattled parapet and a small spire. The south porch is made of Tudor bricks and dates from about 1580.

Inside the church on the right hand side of the choir is a holy water stoup. There is a rather musty atmosphere; this is due to the lingering smell of incense in all principle church services, such as mass.

The organ started to play and we sang 'Ye Holy Angels Bright' — the organ which was formerly a barrel organ was purchased for £60 in 1900.

Father — went up to the altar, which had two large candles, one on each side of it, crossed himself and began:

' Let us pray. The Lord's Prayer. Our Father which art in Heaven —'

'I feel sick,' said a little boy behind me. So there was a shuffle of chairs and the little boy's mother took him out.

The service went on for an hour with singing and prayers. The choirboys then went out in their shining white surplices, one spreading incense as he went out. Followed by Father — blinking more than ever.

AFTERWORD 1990

Mostly, they were recognisable. 'You haven't changed either,' said members of the class of 1960 tactfully. But what took them a little while to appreciate was that they themselves were now considerably older than most of their teachers had been. 'Yes,' they conceded, 'you think your teacher is about a hundred, don't you?' Yes, again. When I was their teacher I was twice their age, but the age gap between us now can be seen clearly for what it always was: little more than the fourteen years covered by their autobiographies.

It was a reunion of staff and students who had started at this school, one of the last purpose-built sec mods, when it opened in 1960. The girls at fourteen had been more like their adult selves, as you'd expect, while thin little boys were yet to fill out and shoot up and otherwise metamorphose: one young man who had had a difficult time with the school, and it with him, was now a changed character – freely remarked on – for love of a good woman (I remember the nice, serious girl). Other personalities were constant. One enthusiastic pupil had become an even more enthusiastic teacher (who had used *Fourteen* in his work – and was keen to emphasise the continuity).

Non-academic members of this, in theory, exclusively non-academic school – though it was 'streamed' – had shrewdly prospered in an increasingly entrepreneurial society. Struggling smallholdings had become profitable garden centres. There was also the odd Ph D and plenty of business diplomas. One member of the original staff remained. He had been in his first teaching post and now, thirty years on, was deputy head. Others from my time had taught there continuously until retirement.

Not having been employed by schools since 1963, I felt some envy at, or sentimental regard for, the understanding of and place in the local community which was the reward of those of my former colleagues who had stuck it out. Twenty-seven years' work with a shifting student population has left me, in that regard, with less.

Here, a number of former pupils told me by way of greeting that they still possessed the exercise-book-length autobiographies they had written in 1961 or 1962. My choosing to end the 1965 selection of their work with Marilyn's 'I would have forgotten about this book long ago' was probably always a piece of propitiatory magic put there in hopes that their writing would continue to live for the authors.

Re-reading the selection evokes an era which was pre-high tech and pre-systems analysis. That is the case with respect not only to the content of the writing but also to the character of the project. My innocent 1965 Introduction to the collection suggests that the writers had no 'problem of *what* to write' because they were dealing with their own lives. Leaving aside the process of discovering within those lives what might be likely to produce good writing (and here the feedback sessions would help) there were decisions which had to be made by the writers (just as much as by an editor) about what to leave out — about ways of recording and structuring experience. Previous class work on linking and distancing thoughts and on the function of chapter and flashback, which it did not occur to me to mention in the 1965 collection (bar a reference to C Day Lewis's *The Otterbury Incident*), would have had some effect on the form and therefore on the content of some of what was written. However, it is quite true that once the original impetus had been achieved the writers were undistracted by teacher during the writing.

The best of the work retains its immediacy, and the recurrent themes – belonging, loss, love, fear – transcend period. However, there is a gulf between then and now: this was the last generation uninfluenced by television in early childhood. I suppose it may have been mentioned in some of the life-stories, but not much. Certainly, the medium produced no comment worth rescuing.

The recollections go back to the late 1940s, to bomb-sites, gas-light, mass tonsillectomy. The weather does seem to be chillier, though there is still an empire (or an Empire Day) on which the sun often shines, teachers are archetypal caners, inter-continental travel is by boat, there are parlour games and electricity cuts, and everybody rides a bike.

Pre-decimal currency outlived the end of the stories, but the post-industrial separateness of towns (sooty) and countryside (leafy) was becoming less tenable. The writers record a blurring of the distinction: 'teeming' ponds filled in, farm cottages allowed to decay, un-made roads tarmacked, new estates built. Pop culture would soon be providing a new version of pastoral, mid-Atlantic, a-seasonal; with (for uncles tended to have one) universal car-ownership just round the corner.

...AND 2008 Donald Measham

There was still bomb damage and other scars of war in their childhood – particularly for those of them who were born in London. I also experienced that. When the RAF bombed Hamburg (Germany's second city) the Luftwaffe — or so it was believed — reacted with hits on the English Midlands.

I was brought up in a newsagent's shop in inner-city Birmingham. By the age of seven my productions included a weekly comic with deadlines. The usual stuff of editing the school magazine came later. Eight novels got themselves written over the years, but remained unpublished. Despite encouragement from Angus Wilson, D J Enright, and others, I

117

somehow continued to live in the wrong place and to be unknown to the right people.

Prior to that, a few years in London and Essex[1] (where the 'Fourteen' work really happened) seemed to have done the trick. I had a contract with Hutchinson for *Leaving*. That sold well. And in 1965 I brought out two other books, *English Now and Then* and *Fourteen*.

All three stemmed from the workaholic years at 'Ashley', though not published until I had changed jobs and moved to Matlock. Older students and younger staff were now coming into the colleges – and a sensible change in the law meant we were no longer *in loco parentis* to our students.

I became head of English and Drama at the college, and – with colleagues Tony Rees, Bob Windsor, the painter David Ainley and others – moved to more student-centred work, in which personal writing played a part. That grew into study-days involving staff, students, professional writers, local teachers, members of the general public.

Amongst the more interesting group publications which emerged – comparable to *Fourteen* – was one deriving from a long day's walk in Derbyshire made by D H Lawrence and Jessie Chambers. Their visit was described in *Sons and Lovers*; ours (our re-enactment) in *Lawrence and the Real England*, published for the Lawrence Festival of 1985.

Staple magazine developed from such work. It came to be recognised by (for example) Peter Finch of the Welsh Academy as one of the top little magazines in the country. I ran it day to day and co-edited (with Bob Windsor) for almost twenty years. Together, we read — unpaid — up to 10,000 submissions annually.

---

[1] 'Ashley' is about 8 miles from Southend-on-Sea — which is referred to as 'Southcliff' in the book. 'Roynton' is Rayleigh; 'Stechford', Rochford.

I had retired shortly after *Staple* got established, retired to paint in a hut, travel with my wife Joan, do things with the grandchildren.

However, the writing bug – particularly the computerised writing bug — drove me onto the kitchen table where I'm a tolerated nuisance. It was there that I finally hit on the right form and title for my novel *Jane Austen out of the blue*, pinned my colours to the print-on-demand mast, and published it on-line through Lulu.

I don't doubt that a number of my former pupils are doing much the same — as local historians, genealogists, bloggers, contributors to literary and technical magazines; as autobiographers (of course), as maybe poets and novelists.[1]

There might have been a case for seeking a terrestrial publisher for the present work. However, I have come to relish the freedom – not least that of choosing one's helpers — which internet publication affords. I guess a number of the contributors to *Fourteen* — now fellow-pensioners — recognise this feeling.

Acknowledgements

The Class of 1960, among them the pupil who took the snapshot
(I can see his face, but regret I cannot recall the name).
Once more, Bill Berrett for his overall design;
Jon Measham, again, for comprehensive technical support.
I am indebted to them all – and many others.

---

[1] The first-year pupil whose English work I described as phenomenal kindly wrote to me around 1990. No, he had not become a professional writer but an Art teacher – though he still writes as if he *writes*.

www.ingramcontent.com/pod-product-compliance
Lightning Source LLC
Chambersburg PA
CBHW061449040426
42450CB00007B/1279